Grammar in context

Essays and interviews

Gramsci in context:
Essays and interviews

Edited by Martin Thomas

ISBN-13: 978-1-909639-00-3

Published 2014 by
Workers' Liberty
20E Tower Workshops
Riley Road
London SE1 3DG

020 7394 8923
awl@workersliberty.org
www.workersliberty.org

First edition published 2012 under the title
"Antonio Gramsci: working-class revolutionary.
Essays and interviews". This second edition
includes corrections and the "Gramsci Glossary"
as additional contents.

Printed by Imprint Digital, Exeter EX5 5HY

The essays and the interview collected here discuss the ideas and the politics of Antonio Gramsci (1891-1937), especially in the light of a major recent study of Gramsci, Peter Thomas's book *The Gramscian Moment*. They argue that Gramsci's ideas are best and mostly loyally understood as a contribution to working-class revolutionary socialist battle against the capitalist system which, as the financial crash of 2008 and its sequels show, is as much a system of class exploitation and social destruction as ever.

"The philosophy of praxis... is the expression of these subaltern classes who want to educate themselves in the art of government and who have an interest in knowing all truths, even the unpleasant ones, and in avoiding the... deceptions of the upper class and — even more — their own." (Gramsci, *Further Selections from the Prison Notebooks*, p.395-6)

"The emancipation of the proletariat is not a labour of small account and of little people; only they who can keep their heart strong and their will as sharp as a sword when the general disillusionment is at its worst can be regarded as fighters for the working class or called revolutionaries."
(Gramsci, *Selections from Political Writings 1910-20*, p.349)

Gramsci's life

Martin Thomas

ANTONIO GRAMSCI ARRIVED as a student at Turin University in 1911 and joined the Socialist Party in 1914. He had had a difficult struggle to get to university — his family was poor — and while at university suffered very bad health.

Turin was one of the foremost industrial cities of Italy. Its population had increased from 338,000 to 430,000 between 1901 and 1911, with the growth of the great car factories such as Fiat. Turin and a few other northern cities were, however, the exception in Italy. Overall Italy was not much more industrialised than Russia. Only about 12% of the employed population were industrial workers.

Figures for 1910:

Cotton consumption, kg per head

Russia 3.0, Italy 5.4

Steel production, kg per head

Russia 38, Italy 28

Coal consumption, kg per head

Russia 300, Italy 270

Italy, like Russia, was a country with some big concentrations of advanced, large-scale industry in the midst of a mainly agricultural and backward economy. Italy's agriculture was not more productive than Russia's.

Italy, however, was a more or less developed bourgeois democracy, with the denser structures of civil society typical of bourgeois democracy as against regimes like Russia's Tsarist autocracy. It had been shaped as such in the battles for the unification of Italy between 1859 and 1870. The feudalistic landlord classes of the south had been hegemonised and co-opted by the northern-based bourgeoisie.

Cities were more developed in Italy. In 1910, Russia had two big cities, and they contained about 2% of the country's population. Italy had six, and they contained 9%. 86% of Russia's population was in agriculture, and only 60% of Italy's. This also meant, however, that the industrial city of Turin was less central in Italian politics than the industrial city of St Petersburg in Russian politics. Turin was overshadowed in politics by the much less industrial cities of Rome and Naples. The workers of Turin could be isolated and marginalised in a way that the workers of St Petersburg — or London, or Paris, or Berlin, or Barcelona — could not.

Italy had vastly more small-scale urban crafts, small industry, and services than Russia. The dominant strategy of Italian governments in the early years of the 20th century, under Giovanni Giolitti, was to co-opt northern industrialists, middle classes, and workers by concessions and protectionism, while squeezing without mercy the poverty-stricken southern peasantry (many already dependent on remittances from family members who had migrated to work in the USA or Argentina).

The Turin working class had a history of big struggles. In spring 1906, after a general strike in most of the northern industrial cities, the textile workers of Turin won an eight hour day. In March 1906 Fiat signed a contract recognising the ten hour day and the workers' "Internal Committees" (something like shop stewards' committees).

In summer 1907 a strike for an Internal Committee at Savigliano failed, and in October a protest strike against the shooting of workers in Milan was defeated. In January 1912 a strike for a shorter working week failed, but a 57 hour week was finally won by a 93-day general strike in 1913.

Italy initially stayed out of World War One, and the Italian Socialist Party opposed the war. By the time Italy joined the war on the side of Britain and France in April 1915, war enthusiasm was ebbing everywhere, and the Socialist Party continued to oppose the war.

There was a wave of strikes in 1915 against Italy entering the war, and a bigger wave of strikes, with street-fighting, in August 1917. But the Socialist Party responded passively, rather than fighting to extend the strikes and bring them to victory.

By this time Gramsci was working as a journalist on the local Socialist Party press. He welcomed the October 1917 Bolshevik revolution, writing:

"The Bolshevik revolution is a revolution against Marx's Capital. *In Russia,* Capital *had more influence among the bourgeoisie than among the proletariat. It demonstrated critically how by fatal necessity a bourgeoisie would be constituted in Russia, how a capitalist era would be inaugurated there, how Western-style civilisation would flourish there, long before the proletariat could even think of its own liberation, of its own class interests, of its own revolution...* [This is an exaggerated reference to the role of "legal Marxists" like Struve who took

Marx's theory one-sidedly as a celebration of the progressive role of capitalism, and became important figures in bourgeois liberal politics].

"The Bolsheviks have denied Karl Marx, and they have affirmed by their actions, by their conquests, that the laws of historical materialism are less inflexible than was hitherto believed." [1]

The Socialist Party was dominated by the so-called "maximalist" faction, led by Giacinto Serrati. They made many loud calls for revolution — and sincere ones, too: Serrati would end up in the Communist Party — but could see no way of developing workers' struggles towards that revolution other than strengthening the Party and waiting for capitalism to collapse through economic crisis.

In March 1919 the whole Socialist Party voted to affiliate to the Communist International. Not even the reformist right wing — a small minority led by Turati, who however controlled the SP group in Parliament — dared oppose affiliation. The main left-wing faction in the SP was led by Amadeo Bordiga, an activist in Naples. Bordiga's concept of revolution depended on building up an intransigent Communist Party around an "invariant doctrine". If the Communist Party stuck to the "invariant doctrine", then the masses would eventually come to it, and the Party would seize power. Otherwise the party would just bolster up reformist solutions for the bourgeoisie. Up to mid-1920, Bordiga's most immediate practical quarrel with Serrati was that Bordiga opposed socialist participation in elections, while Serrati supported it.

Later, in his prison notebooks, Gramsci would write that in 1917 he was still "tendentially somewhat Crocean" [2] — that is, influenced by Benedetto Croce, an idealist philosopher; politically liberal; one of Italy's best-known Italian intellectual figures from the 1890s to the early 1950s; semi-Hegelian; once vaguely sympathetic to Marxism; credited by Eduard Bernstein as a shaping influence in Bernstein's development of "revisionism". But the 1917 article represented a groping towards a more activist, interventionist conception of revolutionary politics than that of the main SP factions.

In April 1919 Gramsci and a few others founded a new socialist paper for Turin, *Ordine Nuovo.* Gramsci wrote later: *"The sentiment that united us... was the sentiment aroused by a vague passion for a vague proletarian culture. We wanted to* do *something..."* They began to ask: *"Is there any germ, a vague hope or hint of... Soviet-style self-government in Italy, in Turin?"* [3]

Gramsci answered yes. The germ was there in the Internal Committees.

The Internal Committees did not look promising as embryo Soviets. They were normally nominated by the trade union officials, and they ignored the numerous workers who were not trade union members.

In June 1919 *Ordine Nuovo* started its campaign for the Internal Committees to be transformed into factory councils, elected by the whole workforce. In September 1919 the first factory council was founded, at the Brevetti branch of the Fiat complex. By 26 October, 50,000 workers were represented by factory councils; by the end of the year, 150,000.

Gramsci wrote: *"For ourselves and our followers,* L'Ordine Nuovo *became 'the journal of the factory councils'."* [4]

"The factory council is the model of the proletarian state. All the problems inherent in the organisation of the proletarian state are inherent in the organisation of the council.

"In the one as in the other, the concept of citizen gives way to the concept of the comrade... Everyone is indispensable; everyone is at his post; and everyone has a function and a post.

"Even the most ignorant and backward of the workers, even the most vain and 'civil' of engineers, eventually convinces himself of this truth in the experience of factory organisation. All eventually acquire a communist consciousness that enables them to comprehend what a great step forward the communist economy represents over the capitalist..." [5]

The right wing and the centre of the Socialist Party were cool on the factory councils because they saw them as cutting across union organisation. Bordiga was cool because he saw the factory councils project as a syndicalistic diversion from fighting for state power. He was not *entirely* a prisoner of dogma. The almost-exclusive orientation to the factory councils in the big metal-working factories, where almost all workers were male, meant a lack of attention to other sections of the working class, including most working-class women.

The big metal-working factories were, however, the biggest working-class concentrations in Italy. In April 1920, they led a huge general strike in Turin. The Socialist Party did not organise a campaign to support the workers, and they were defeated.

In June the workers were in struggle again, occupying the factories and continuing production under workers' management. The Socialist Party delegated the task of doing something about the occupations to the leading trade union officials. The union officials organised a referendum in September 1920, posing the question as immediate revolution or negotiations.

A small majority voted for negotiations, and the occupations were defeated. Gramsci wrote: *"The emancipation of the proletariat is not a labour of small account and of little people; only they who can keep their hearts strong and their will as sharp as a sword when the general disillusionment is at its worst can be regarded as fighters for the working class or called revolutionaries".* [6]

The workers' defeat opened the way for the rise of fascism. Mussolini would take power in October 1922 and consolidate it by 1926. Much remained in the balance over the six years between 1920 and 1926. Gramsci set about trying to shape a new Italian Communist Party to weigh in the balance.

Some of the ideas he would bring in to that battle had already been shaped in his editing of the paper *Ordine Nuovo*. Gramsci saw the common run of socialist journalism in his time as agitational, simplistic, bombastic, economistic. *Ordine Nuovo* was much more reflective. He conceived of it as "a communist cultural review".

"We have... set out what we believe a paper, a communist cultural review, should be. Such a paper must aim to become, in miniature, complete in itself, and, even though it may be unable to satisfy all the intellectual needs of the nucleus of men who read and support it, who live a part of their lives around it, and who impart to it some of their own life, it must strive to be the kind of journal in which everyone will find things that interest and move him, that will lighten the daily burden of work, economic struggle, and political discussion.

"At the least, the journal should encourage the complete development of one's mental capacities for a higher and fuller life, richer in harmony and in ideological aims, and should be a stimulus for the development of one's own personality." [7]

"The workers loved Ordine Nuovo *(this we can state with inner satisfaction), and why did they love it? Because in its articles they rediscovered a part, the best part, of themselves. Because they felt that its articles were permeated with that same spirit of inner searching that they experienced: 'How can we become free? How can we become ourselves?'*

"Because its articles were not cold intellectual structures, but sprang from our discussions with the best workers; they elaborated the actual sentiments, goals, and passions of the Turin working class, that we ourselves had provoked and tested. Because its articles were virtually a 'taking note' of actual events, seen as moments of a process of inner liberation and self-expression on the part of the working class. This is why the workers loved L'Ordine Nuovo, *and how its idea came to be formed."* [8]

After the Second Congress of the Communist International, in 1920,

Bordiga accepted the policy of the International in favour of taking part in elections. The chief issue between him and Serrati came to be that of splitting the Socialist Party.

Bordiga wanted to split quickly and form a hard Communist Party, however small. Serrati wanted to continue with a united party, though he admitted that the worst reformists would eventually have to be expelled.

In May 1920, Gramsci wrote a document entitled *Towards the Renewal of the Socialist Party*. He warned: *"The present phase... in Italy... precedes either the conquest of political power on the part of the revolutionary proletariat... or a tremendous reaction on the part of the propertied classes and governing caste... a bid to smash once and for all... the Socialist Party and to incorporate... the trade unions... into the machinery of the bourgeois state"*.

In response: *"The* [party] *leadership... must become the motor centre for proletarian action in all its manifestations... Communist groups in all factories, unions, etc.... will develop the propaganda needed to conquer the unions, the Chambers of Labour* [like Trades Councils] *and the General Confederation of Labour in an organic fashion, and so become the trusted elements whom the masses will delegate to form political Soviets and exercise the proletarian dictatorship"*. [9]

The document was praised by Lenin and the Bolshevik leaders, who read it from afar, in Moscow. But from then to 1922, Gramsci largely went along with Bordiga. He made no attempt to organise a distinct faction outside Turin.

In January 1921 Bordiga finally forced through a split. It was messy. The Socialist Party had had 216,000 members in 1920. After the split the Socialist Party (Serrati-Turati) and the Communist Party had fewer than 100,000 members between them. In 1922 the Socialist Party expelled the reformists, and in 1924, under pressure from the Communist International and against Bordiga's protests, the "Terzini" faction of the Socialist Party, led by Serrati, was separated from the Socialist Party and joined the Communist Party.

The fascist movement grew at enormous speed after the workers' defeat in 1920. The bourgeoisie, frightened after 1920, and faced with economic depression in 1921-2, gave it support. Significant numbers of pre-1914 syndicalist militants rallied to the fascist leader Mussolini, who was himself a former member of the Socialist Party.

In October 1922 Mussolini took power. At first he went cautiously, not even changing the constitution for two years. In May 1924 the reformist-Socialist parliamentary deputy Giacomo Matteotti was murdered after openly denouncing Mussolini in Parliament. In the months that followed, the fascist regime was shaken by mass revolt. But it weathered the storm, and in October 1926 imposed the "Exceptional Laws" which stamped out all labour movement and political activity.

"The Italian Communist Party came into being almost simultaneously with fascism. But the same conditions of revolutionary ebb tide, which carried the fascists to power, served to deter the development of the Communist Party.

"It did not give itself an accounting as to the full sweep of the fascist danger; it lulled itself with revolutionary illusions; it was irreconcilably antagonistic to the policy of the united front; in short, it was stricken with all the infantile diseases.

"Small wonder! It was only two years old. In its eyes, fascism appeared to be only 'capitalist reaction'. The particular *traits of fascism which spring from the mobilization of the petty bourgeoisie against the proletariat, the Communist Party was unable to discern. Italian comrades inform me that, with the sole exception of Gramsci, the Communist Party would not even allow for the possibility of the fascists' seizing power..."* (Trotsky, writing in 1932). [10]

There was confusion not only in the Italian Communist Party but also in the International. Stalin and Zinoviev declared that fascism and social democracy were "twins".

Gramsci failed to fight for his analysis against Bordiga. In summer 1921 workers had spontaneously formed anti-fascist defence squads. Bordiga condemned these squads as a diversion from the proper task of the revolutionary party, and a taking of sides in an internal quarrel of the bourgeoisie with which workers had no concern. The fight against fascism was inseparable from the fight against the bourgeoisie as a whole, and must be led by the CP.

The Socialist Party also opposed the defence squads, advocating peaceful resistance. Gramsci seems to have disagreed with Bordiga, yet he did not support the small faction in the CP, led by Angelo Tasca, which argued for support for the defence squads and for a general policy of united front action.

Bordiga opposed the "united front" policy of the Communist International, other than in the trade-union sphere, where he accepted it. In March 1922 his view was codified by the Communist Party, in the "Rome Theses". Gramsci voted for the Rome Theses, though later he would explain his vote as an attempt to avoid disrupting the party.

In mid-1922 Gramsci went to Russia for the Fourth Congress of the Communist International; after the Congress he stayed on as resident member of the Executive of the International, although much of the time he was out of action through ill health. He married Julia Schucht, a Russian. In Russia Gramsci was won over to the policy of the united front. Early in 1923, the fascist government in Italy arrested Bordiga and other prominent leaders of the Italian CP. In June 1923 the Executive of the International decided to reconstitute the CP leadership from outside, and from September Gramsci became the effective leader of the party, operating from Vienna together with other people from the former *Ordine Nuovo* group.

The process of trying to reorient the party was complicated by the fact that the degeneration of the Communist International had already begun. In the "Lyons Theses" drafted by Gramsci and Palmiro Togliatti, and adopted by the CP in January 1926, Comintern policy on "Bolshevisation" was followed to include a ban on factions within the CP.

Still, Gramsci restated his claim for an interventionist party, against Bordigism. *"Only as a consequence of its action among the masses can the Party obtain recognition as 'their' Party"*. [11] The Lyons Theses also included a social-historical analysis of Italy, particularly of the "Southern Question", and of fascism. In May 1924 Gramsci returned to Italy. He was able to operate for a while with the legal privileges of a member of parliament. In November 1926 the fascist government put him in jail, and would keep him there until a few days before his death in 1937.

For most of his ten years in prison Gramsci was seriously ill. For most of it he was also isolated (though early on he was in the same jail as Bordiga and the two of them, personally friendly, shared the task of organising lectures and seminars for the other political prisoners). He depended heavily for his contact with the outside world on his friend Piero Sraffa (by then a professor of economics at Cambridge) and his sister-in-law Tatiana Schucht. His wife Julia suffered a nervous breakdown and would let months or years pass by without writing to him.

In prison Gramsci decided, as he put it, to do something "für ewig", for the long term, and wrote 2848 pages of *Prison Notebooks*, dealing with philosophy; education; intellectuals and politics; Italian history; economism and the character of a revolutionary party; the organisation of political "hegemony"; "Fordism"; world economic trends; criticism of Croce; trends in Catholicism; and other issues.

Much of the language of the *Prison Notebooks* was cryptic, making it easier in later years for the Italian CP and then a whole swathe of "post-Marxist" intellectuals to "appropriate" Gramsci. But a more loyal reading of the *Prison Notebooks* will see them as continuing to explore the ideas and goals of Gramsci before 1926.

"*One attempt to start a revision of the current tactical methods*", he wrote, "*was perhaps that outlined by* [Trotsky] *at the* [Fourth World Congress], *when he made a comparison between the Eastern and Western fronts. The former had fallen at once, but unprecedented struggles had then ensued; in the case of the latter, the struggles would occur 'beforehand'...*" [12]

This would be interpreted by the Italian CP as indicating a struggle to win working-class hegemony in "civil society" — for example, by controlling city councils — bit by bit over a long period. What Gramsci meant was a longer process of united front tactics, of winning bases of support in the working class and influence in other plebeian sectors, of the sort he had sketched in his 1920 document on the "Renewal of the Socialist Party".

"[Lenin]... *did not have time to expand his formula* [of the united front] — *though it should be remembered that he could only have expanded it theoretically, whereas the fundamental task was a national one; that is to say, it demanded a reconnaissance of the terrain and identification of the elements of trench and fortress represented by the elements of civil society, and so on...*

"*The State was only an outer ditch, behind which there was a powerful system of fortresses and earthworks: more or less numerous from one State to the next, it goes without saying* — *but this precisely necessitated an accurate reconnaissance of each individual country.*" [13]

In other words, bourgeois rule rested on a vast complex of social institutions and networks. In many countries, though Gramsci did not make this explicit, it rests on bureaucratised labour movements locked into a "loyal opposition" configuration. The simple-minded approach, typical of many factions of Italian socialism before Gramsci, of agitation through superficial scandal-mongering against the bourgeoisie and championing the elementary economic demands of the working class, was inadequate in the face of such an enemy. Lenin's idea of the revolutionary party as "a tribune of the people" was vital. The working class must educate itself as a future ruling class; organise on a whole series of levels; and show itself as a potential leader to the rest of the plebeian population (in Italy, the peasantry), before it could defeat the bourgeoisie.

Gramsci condemned traditional Italian socialism sharply for its attitude to the peasantry of the south (the "Southern Question"). As Gramsci had written in an unpublished article of November 1926:

"*It is well known what ideology is propagated through the multifarious forms of bourgeois propaganda among the masses of the North: The South is a lead weight which impedes a more rapid civil development of Italy; the southerners are biologically inferior beings, semi-barbarians, or complete barbarians, by natural destiny. If the South is backward, the fault is not to be found in the capitalist system or in any other historical cause, but is the fault of nature... The Socialist Party was largely the vehicle for this bourgeois ideology among the northern proletariat".* [14]

The question had concerned Gramsci since his first socialist activity in 1914. In that same year, 1914, *"there had occurred in Turin an episode which potentially contained all the action and propaganda developed in the post-war period by the Communists".* [15]

The Turin socialists proposed to back Gaetano Salvemini for parliamentary deputy. Salvemini was a liberal rather than a socialist, but also the chief public champion of the southern peasantry. The Turin socialists wanted to use their control of a parliamentary "safe seat" — landlords, mafia, and the Church had electoral hegemony in the South — to give Salvemini a voice in parliament and demonstrate their support for the southern peasantry.

Salvemini did not stand, but he did speak publicly in support of the Socialist candidate.

For those who want to make Gramsci a pioneer of "Popular Front" tactics, it should be noted that the Turin socialists added: *"The workers of Turin... will carry on their propaganda according to their principles and will not be at all committed by the political activity of Salvemini".* [13]

Gramsci summed up the approach he was trying to develop as follows, in another article from the 1920s:

"The metalworkers, the joiners, the builders, etc., must not only think as proletarians and no longer as metalworkers, joiners, or builders, but they must take a step forward: they must think as members of a class which aims at leading the peasants and intellectuals, of a class which can conquer and can build socialism only if aided and followed by the great majority of these social strata. If it does not do this, the proletariat does not become a leading class, and these strata, which represent in Italy the majority of the population, remain under bourgeois leadership, and give the State the possibility of resisting and weakening the proletarian attack." [16]

Gramsci centred his adult life, and much of his theoretical effort while in prison, on the building of a Marxist party. In his prison notebooks he spelled out how and why such a party must be a constantly self-educating organisation rather than Bordiga's idea of one structured by "organic centralism" around what Bordiga called "the invariant doctrine".

"[With] a rigid and rigorously formulated doctrinal system... is there a 'guarantee' of immutability? No, there is not. Formulas will be recited by heart without changing an iota, but real activity will be quite different. One must... conceive of 'ideology'... historically, as an incessant struggle. Organic centralism imagines it can construct once and for all an organism that is objectively perfect right from the start. This illusion can be dangerous..."

"A collective consciousness, a living organism, is formed only after the unification of the multiplicity through friction on the part of the individuals... An orchestra tuning-up, every instrument playing by itself, sounds a most hideous cacophony, yet these warm-ups are the necessary condition for the orchestra to come to life as a single 'instrument'..." [17]

The party must not be a walled-off sect whose special jargon serves to insulate from intellectual challenge from outside.

"Everything that is not expressed in their language is a delirium, a prejudice, a superstition, etc..." [18] He found *"many traces of this tendency"* not just in Bordiga, but in the *Popular Manual*, a text by Nikolai Bukharin from 1921. Just before being jailed, Gramsci himself had planned to organise the Italian Communist Party's political education around Bukharin's text, but in prison he wrote a thorough criticism of it, the longest relatively finished section of his notebooks.

The revolutionary Marxist party must always seek for political initiative and for the intellectual and political high ground. It must not be content just to build up organisational strength through crude scandal-mongering and economistic agitation, and to wait for capitalist crisis to rally the workers behind it.

"Statistical laws can be employed in the science and art of politics only so long as the great masses of the population remain... essentially passive... [But] political action tends precisely to rouse the masses from passivity, in other words to destroy the law of large numbers... In reality one can 'scientifically' foresee only the struggle, but not the concrete moments of the struggle...

"One can 'foresee' to the extent that one acts, to the extent that one applies a voluntary effort and therefore contributes concretely to creating the result 'foreseen'. Prediction reveals itself thus not as a scientific act of knowledge, but as the abstract expression of the effort made, the practical way of creating a collective will." [19]

The philosophy of praxis

A presentation by *Peter Thomas* of the basic themes of his book *The Gramscian Moment*.

I'LL START BY TALKING roughly about what motivated me to write this book, and then talk briefly about some of the theses, particularly related to questions of political strategy and political organisations.

Gramsci is today one of the most widely-known theorists from what we might call, in abbreviated form, the "golden age" of Marxism. I hesitate to use the term "classical Marxism", but I'm speaking in terms of the early years of Marxism through the Second International and into the early years of the Third International. He is one of the authors who has survived the last period of negative, anti-Marxist sentiment in universities and in culture more generally – certainly more so than Engels and probably even more so than Marx himself. He's taught on university courses in a whole variety of areas, from the humanities across to social sciences and political theory, history, philosophy, sociology, anthropology and literary criticism; for many young people today, I expect Gramsci is one of the first Marxist authors they'll encounter. There are positives and negatives involved in this process and this reputation of Gramsci.

One of the reasons that Gramsci is so widely known today and has survived a long period that many other Marxist authors did not is because of a particular interpretation of Gramsci that was developed in the 1970s and associated with the Eurocommunists in particular, and later with certain tendencies that flowed into what you could call the New Labour culture here in Britain and internationally. That presented a very contentious picture of Gramsci, which was namely the idea that Gramsci represented a break with what you could call a certain Leninist heritage, or the heritage associated with the October Revolution, and that Gramsci focused on questions of culture, of ideas, of superstructure and neglected some of the themes — particularly the critique of political economy — that had been central for earlier Marxist theorists.

That was the fundamental image I received as a young student when I first started reading Gramsci. But from my own reading of Gramsci, and from comments from older comrades who remembered different times, I had some sense that there was something not quite right with this picture. Something didn't quite work. I became very interested in exploring Gramsci's thought further. That set me off on a long path of research into many different areas of Gramsci's thought, which has finally resulted in the publication of this book. The fundamental thesis of this book is that Gramsci remains a thinker committed to a particular current that emerged from the October Revolution and attempted to reformulate a very sophisticated version of Marxism — both in terms of a theory of political activity and a broader "conception of the world." This book contests a very widespread image of Gramsci as representing a break with the Leninist tradition, or at least one element of a certain Leninist tradition.

One element of this study was critically confronting some of the perspectives that were presented in a very important and influential article by Perry Anderson in *New Left Review* in 1976. Anderson's argument in this article was that the Eurocommunist appropriation of Gramsci's thought which had occurred in the preceding years and continued well on to the 70s and 80s was a betrayal of Gramsci's thought, but was not entirely unwarranted on the basis of the notebooks that Gramsci wrote when he was in prison. That is to say, Anderson proposed the thesis that while in prison, and writing his most well-known work the *Prison Notebooks*, Gramsci had undertaken a slow slide in which various difficulties to which he was subjected had led him to forget some of the fundamental insights of Marx, Engels and Lenin regarding the nature of state power , the nature of the capitalist state and the necessary forms of political organisation of a proletarian movement. When I first read this study, I was very impressed with the depth and the vision that was offered of Gramsci's thought. Anderson's argument depended on tracking a certain transmutation in Gramsci's thought over his years of incarceration, particularly regarding the concept of hegemony. Anderson tracks a steady transformation by reading the critical edition of the *Prison Notebooks*, which had just been published in 1975, whereby Gramsci forgets the nature of the coercive power of the bourgeoisie and instead conceives of "hegemony", which is posited in a neutral sense, merely as a technique of political organisation that either the bourgeoisie or the working class can adopt, which is really a conceptual power which is not in any real sense political, but occurs only at the pre-political level of civil society.

As I read further into the critical *Notebooks*, however, I noticed certain discrepancies to do with the basic philological infrastructure of this reading. For example, the sequence of texts that Anderson analysed appear to be in chronological order. But when one goes further into the *Notebooks* and sees the way in which Gramsci had written them, under very difficult conditions, one realises that in fact some of the texts Anderson posited as coming later had come before the initial texts that he quoted. Therefore, the very sequential narrative that was recounted didn't hold. We needed another way of trying to understand the development and progression of Gramsci's thought

When I delved further into Gramsci's pre-prison writings, about his period of activity in the Italian Communist Party, I began to believe that the period of time he spent in the Soviet Union and his attendance at the Fourth Congress of the Third International was decisive for his political development, which progressed through the 1920s and reached a certain composition under very difficult conditions while in prison in the 1930s; fundamentally, this was the perspective of the united front.

So when Gramsci visits the Soviet Union and attends the Fourth Congress of the Third International, he encounters a particular conception of the united front which is very different from some other explanations of the concept. This enables him to grasp the way in which a mass basis of politics becomes the precondition for any genuine revolutionary movement in the West. I also began to think that the way Gramsci had been presented as a "Western Marxist", a break with the Leninist tradition, was not in fact reflected in the texts themselves. Many of the themes emerging from the *Prison Notebooks* could be found in the discussions of Lenin and Trotsky. I therefore attempted to think through Gramsci's theory not as a supposedly "Western" response to an "Eastern" or "classical" Marxism, but rather as the attempt to translate — a term that Gramsci, who was trained initially at university as a linguist, uses himself — some of the theoretical gains that he found in the practical politics of the post-revolutionary period in the Soviet Union. He was attempting first to translate them into a principle for understanding the rise of bourgeois hegemony, and secondly to attempt to think through some of the principles of political action he found in Lenin's thought that he could develop into a theory and practice of what I call in the book "proletarian hegemony".

This also leads into quite a lengthy discussion of the status of Marxism in relation to philosophy. This may not be focused on political questions, but I think that, in terms of Gramsci's thought, it's important to emphasise this element. It connects very closely with the way he develops the concept of hegemony. Philosophy for Gramsci was not concerned with particular technical questions; the tradition he'd inherited from Italian Marxism, and also from Italian bourgeois philosophers such as Benedetto Croce, meant that he was very concerned with practical philosophy as a conception of the world; in Marxist terms, an ideology. Not as an illusion, but as a system of ideas that are used and organised to achieve certain practical effects.

Gramsci therefore comes to be convinced, during his period in prison, that there's a need to elaborate Marxism as a philosophy of praxis. This was not a word he used simply as a code-word to escape the eyes of the censor; he had substantive reasons for doing so. He became convinced that one of the forms in which the bourgeoisie had been able to establish its dominance had been a pre-eminently philosophical process in which there was a continuing separation of *organisation* and *association* — that is, *organisation* from above by a very restricted class, and the *association* of the masses from below. Gramsci thinks that, to confront this type of split in culture — which occurs on a global scale and is a product of capitalism's innate requirement for a split between those who manage and appropri-ate, and those who work and associate — there was a need to challenge the underlying conception of philosophy and human thought with a phi-losophy of praxis. This would emphasise that philosophy and ideas — instances of organisation, if you like; very complicated conceptual lin-guistic forms – need to be understood themselves as practical activities. We don't have metaphysics on the one hand and the sullen terrestrial terrain underneath it, which is given its truth by theology. Instead we need to be thoroughly secular and bring truth down and posit truth itself as a practical element in the organisation of social relations. So that's a very direct attack precisely on the division of labour that's organised as a class relation in the production process.

Gramsci develops this conception of Marxism to combat what he sees as possible bureaucratic deformations in the development of Marxism throughout its history and particularly in the period which he's writing. He then builds this into his analysis of different forms of hegemony; he sees bourgeois hegemony as fundamentally dedicated to the organisation of particularly coercive layers of consent. He talks about consent being coercively extracted from what he calls the "popular layers" of society — if you like, ordinary people, the working class. This is done precisely in order to pacify them. Gramsci links this very closely in his discussions with the critique of political economy. This involves both a historical discussion — including a discussion of various elements of the legacy of Ricardo, which he conducts with his friend Piero Sraffa — as well as very close attention to some of the debates in Marx's political and economic theory at the time. He is also very concerned to work out what would be a genuine proletarian hegemony. Certain indicators and signposts in the *Prison Notebooks* are hard to decipher. We're not so much subject to censorship either by Gramsci himself or an external censor; Gramsci was not in fact that restricted in what he could write in prison. We're more subject to the nature of these writings being notes that he hopes to elaborate later. His health didn't permit him to do so; he died shortly after release from prison.

He never had the chance to develop his notes into a full study. Looking closely, though, you can see indications of how these ideas begin to link up with his earlier experiences from the Fourth Congress. He seems to have understood that the word "hegemony" had undergone a transformation from the pre-revolutionary situation, where it had been developed by Lenin in particular to indicate the leading relationship of the industrial working class to the peasantry. This relationship was decisive to the success of the revolution in the Soviet Union. It becomes very different in the period of the New Economic Policy and assumes very complicated forms. Gramsci believes that the cultural politics of Lenin at the time of the NEP are very interesting in terms of conceiving of a mass base for a united front, which could draw together — from the base — not only the exploited classes but also the oppressed classes; the "popular layers", all those who were not capitalists or exploiters or aristocrats.

What he sees in this in particular is the attempt by what we might call the "last" Lenin to develop a political culture in which participation was an available possibility for all members of society, within the very severe limits that had been imposed by the years of the civil war. Lenin's support for literacy programmes after the civil war is now tragically forgotten, but it was one of his main concerns for precisely political reasons — that is, to enable a mass base for participation in post-civil war reconstruction. It was also about developing, for what remained of the industrial working class, a political consciousness of the need to provide a genuine leadership to society. That leadership had to enable masses of people previously excluded from public life to participate actively in decision-making processes.

Gramsci grasps upon this as a form of "active" hegemony. It is not simply coercive, in the sense of extracting consent from people, but wins their active support and in so doing makes them more active. There's a certain energising element to what Gramsci posits as a possible dimension of proletarian hegemony.

One of the other elements that this all ultimately flows into is something which also goes against one of the most dominant images of Gramsci. That is that all of Gramsci's researches begin with a concern for forms of political organisation. As he develops his thoughts, and turns in his studies to considering the very radical nature of Machiavelli's political theory, he begins to develop the notion of "the modern prince". This becomes, according to some people, merely Gramsci's codeword for "the political party", however understood. But in the context of what Gramsci is trying to do, considering the way he tries to reconnect to the level of democratic pedagogy in Lenin's political theory both before the Russian Revolution and also under very difficult circumstances in the period after the civil war, we can see that "the modern prince" for Gramsci is not merely a euphemism for actually existing political parties but becomes Gramsci's concrete proposal for the type of political party that would be needed to continue what we might call the Leninist challenge. The "modern prince" becomes the central element of his thought, and we cannot present a picture of Gramsci – who is essentially killed by the fascists for being the leader of a working-class organisation – as somehow representing a break with forms of political organisation and drifting off into a vague cultural or pre-cultural critique or merely dissent.

Gramsci sees the figure of "the modern prince" as the type of organisation that would allow for the debates that need to happen, the points of disagreement, the composition of alliances and new perspectives – an ongoing process, as it were, of self-education, of people engaged in forms of organising themselves rather than being organised by others. There's a break with a bureaucratic conception, which Gramsci himself had been susceptible to, and Gramsci's attempt to think through the way the political party in his period could be conceived not as an instrument of bureaucratic control or command but a space or site in which a new civilisation of values are developed. For Gramsci, this means the concrete activity of organising in different forms.

This goes a long way beyond the type of things to which politics has been reduced in our own period, largely due to the lack of the mass base that would be needed to make these ideas meaningful in a concrete sense. Gramsci is talking about developing an entire infrastructure of social relations that would prepare the way for the self-education of the working classes to participate actively in politics. Ultimately, against the image that I received as a young student of Gramsci as a departure from a directly political Marxism, we need to reaffirm that deepening conception of politics and political organisation – and linking that with a Marxist critique of political economy – remains at the absolute centre of Gramsci's project the entire way through.

The ultimate legacy he gives us is then trying to conceive of the ways in which political organisation are theoretical in their own forms, and also the ways in which theory is a form of political organisation. There's a strong red line of emphasis on the primacy of politics that runs through Gramsci's thought, which doesn't in any sense negate the fundamental principles of the materialist conception of history. There's an attempt to rethink the concrete forms in which the materialist conception of history and the critique of political economy can move from being the preserve of small groups of people to becoming the base for a genuine mass culture and civilisation.

That, for me, is why Gramsci remains a point of connection to the past of the Marxist tradition as well as a fundamental point for trying to reorganise and recompose a Marxism that can take this position, and that can flourish and grow as a genuine culture in wider society.

"Ideas for Freedom" weekend school, 28-29 November 2009

"The Gramscian Moment": an interview with Peter Thomas

The following interview with Peter Thomas about his book *The Gramscian Moment* **was conducted by Martin Thomas in stages over a period of about three years.**

"HEGEMONIC APPARATUS"

You argue that Gramsci's discussion of "hegemony" is more political and class-based than those who interpret the idea as a diffuse striving for cultural influence would admit, and moreover is crystallised in a project of a "hegemonic apparatus". You explain Gramsci's idea of "hegemonic apparatus" in this way. "A class's hegemonic apparatus is the wide-ranging series of institutions (understood in the broadest sense) and practices — from newspapers to educational organisations to political parties – by means of which a class and its allies engage their opponents in a struggle for political power... the means by which a class's forces in civil society are translated into power in political society".

In that sense, however, the working class does not have a hegemonic apparatus in any country in the world. There is class struggle, there are institutions based in the working class where that struggle takes place, but no "hegemonic apparatus". What guidance does the idea of "hegemonic apparatus", or of united front, give us in this situation? Or again, take the strongest ever revolutionary working-class party to exist in a capitalist country, the German Communist

Party of the early 1920s. It was very decidedly a minority in the trade unions, and not clearly a majority in the factory councils. The united front tactic was about contesting those areas. The unions, for example, were not part of a "hegemonic apparatus" as something already set up and strategically integrated. What would the idea of "hegemonic apparatus" indicate about what to do in the unions?

It's useful to come back to another question: in what way did Gramsci further develop the idea of hegemony? It's important to note that Gramsci derives the concept of hegemony directly from the debates in Russian Social Democracy, where it meant a leading position of the working class in relation to the peasantry in the context of a democratic revolution against Tsarism. It is also important, and sometimes not noted, that Gramsci also develops the post-revolutionary concept of hegemony, as it was elaborated by Lenin in particular.

Hegemony, in the Russian context, is used continuously by Lenin as a synonym for political leadership. Gramsci himself explicitly makes this equation of hegemony with political leadership on numerous occasions throughout the *Prison Notebooks*. He also explicitly refers to the way in which Lenin in his final years had tried to theorise and to develop practically a concept of hegemony that went beyond the earlier debates, one that would indicate a leading role for the Russian working class in the post-revolutionary process.

What Gramsci is referring to there, in a very complicated and difficult form, is the policy that Lenin attempted to outline and to realise after the civil war – what Moshe Lewin describes as "Lenin's last struggle". Under very difficult circumstances, the Russian working class needed to assume the responsibility of political leadership in the process known as the New Economic Policy, a process filled with all sorts of contradictions. Lenin saw the possibility within that process of the Russian working class now not simply leading the peasantry in a struggle against Tsarism, but positing a political programme that could reshape the social relations inside a social formation devastated after the civil war.

On an international level, that battle had an important link to the politics of the united front – the necessity of the politics of the united front, not merely as a tactical consideration, but in a deeper conception of the political potential of the organised working class not only in Russia but internationally.

In the *Prison Notebooks* Gramsci attempts to further develop insights that he believes to see in the political practice of the last Lenin, in particular from the time Gramsci was in the Soviet Union, between June 1922 and November 1923, and during which he was interacting directly with the Bolshevik leadership. The concepts of hegemony and political leadership were of course widespread in the Communist movement of the 1920s. Gramsci was not the only person to develop a theory of hegemony. (Stalin, for example, quite explicitly invoked the category and its "Leninist" heritage; Gramsci was well aware of this attempted inheritance and was highly critical of its vulgarisations and deformations). Gramsci wanted to develop the concept further through reflecting on Lenin's considerations and in particular his political practice.

I think he developed it in two directions. On the one hand, on his return to Italy, and throughout the mid-1920s, when he assumed the leadership of the Communist Party of Italy, in very difficult circumstances, he tried to comprehend what the concept of the united front could mean under fascist rule in Italy. In prison, Gramsci continued that project, in a theoretical form, by considering the possibilities for working-class leadership in the struggle against fascism. In this period of isolation from daily political engagement as a professional revolutionary, Gramsci also attempted to develop the concept of hegemony into what he refers to as a historical-political criterion, a criterion for historical study. He tries to discern the ways in which such a concrete concept of political leadership can be used to throw light back on the long process, the long democratic revolution of modernity and the constitution of the new forms of modern politics.

On the basis of experiences that occurred in the "East" – according to the classic distinction – Gramsci attempts to comprehend the history of the "West". In some sense, the intensity of the Russian revolutionary process had opened up forms and ways of thinking, new concepts for Gramsci, that could help him understand what was specific about democratic politics in its broadest sense in the context of the modern bourgeois state; the way that different social groups attempt to win support and consent; to engage in acts of coercion against their opponents; to expand their own forces while reducing those of their opponents, and so forth.

As he was studying the history of the West, he noted a whole series of practices deployed by the bourgeoisie throughout the "long nineteenth century", from the French Revolution onwards, that were aimed to consolidate its position of political leadership. (For Gramsci, political leadership is not opposed to social or cultural leadership; it necessarily includes those elements and provides their fullest development). He simultaneously retranslates the term hegemony back into a consideration of the kind of hegemony it would be necessary for the working class to build in the West. He finds here many similarities with the forms of association which the bourgeoisie had developed – networks, societies, groups, clubs etc. – but he also finds an important distinction.

He states this difference in very traditional, remarkably classical philosophical terms. Bourgeois hegemony, because it is leadership by a class that needs to conceal the unequal social, economic and juridical relations that lie at the heart of bourgeois claims to formal equality, necessarily engages in distortions and mystifications; a politics of the absence of the truth. For a proletarian hegemony, Gramsci argues that a politics of truth is necessary. He states on many occasions that the precondition for doing mass politics in the working classes is to speak the truth.

"The philosophy of praxis, on the other hand, does not aim at the peaceful resolution of existing contradictions in history and society but is rather the very theory of these contradictions. It is not the instrument of government of the dominant groups in order to gain the consent of and exercise hegemony over the subaltern classes; it is the expression of these subaltern classes who want to educate themselves in the art of government and who have an interest in knowing all truths, even the unpleasant ones, and in avoiding the (impossible) deceptions of the upper class and — even more — their own" [20].

What is necessary for the new forms of democratic associations – of societies, networks, and so forth – capable of functioning is what I call in my book "a dialectical pedagogical relationship". It means forms of proletarian hegemony that would attempt to echo, and deepen, and make even more complex, the forms of hegemony that Lenin in his last years attempted to realise.

It is often forgotten that one of Lenin's last overriding concerns was the need for the Russian working classes to play not only a role in economic reconstruction but also in cultural renovation. The "last" Lenin was concerned, for example, with literacy programmes. Why? Because mass literacy would enable mass participation in politics. He was concerned with the establishment of cultural institutions that would extend the possibility of political relationships and practices, not merely in the city but throughout the countryside, permitting a genuinely democratic participation in political life by all strata of the labouring classes.

His work was dedicated to convincing layers of the working class to take part actively in this process, in a role of leadership. They would then become forces for modernisation and renovation of all the social relations throughout Russian society.

In this sense, there is a very important continuity of Lenin's legacy in Gramsci's thought, both before his imprisonment in his role as leader of the Italian Communist Party but even more intensely, in a theoretical form, in the *Prison Notebooks*.

One of the ways in which Gramsci goes beyond the Russian debates – not only the pre-revolutionary debates, but also the contribution of "the last Lenin" – consists in the development of the concept of a "hegemonic apparatus". This concept, with Gramsci, develops slowly in his work throughout the *Prison Notebooks* project and is equated with different terms on different occasions. One particularly significant one is that of the "material structure" of the superstructures. Gramsci was attempting to think through the way in which the superstructures, as derived from the base-superstructure metaphor, could be conceived of not simply in ideological terms, as ideas and concepts, but quite materially, as practices, relations and institutions. He wanted to look at the way in which these became unified as an articulated system of institutions under the banner of the project of a particular class or social group.

We thus have in Gramsci not only the notion of a hegemonic apparatus, in the singular, but also of hegemonic apparatuses, in the plural – a whole series of hegemonic apparatuses that come together and are unified at the political level by the capacity of elements of a particular social group or class to draw into a dialogue, or, to use Gramsci's term, to "translate" between, different hegemonic practices in different fields of the society.

"REVOLUTIONARY PARTY

A "hegemonic apparatus" is not just a "series of institutions", is it? In the sense of a string of things, one after the other? Doesn't it need to have an internal structure? Doesn't a working-class "hegemonic apparatus" require the development at its centre of a revolutionary political party, shaping and leading the other institutions, trade-unions, community organisations, workers' councils, and so on?

Certainly, we are not dealing with an indifferent series of one thing after another. Gramsci is quite aware that there are different hierarchies and structures and relations between practices. Not all practices are equal to each other, or rather, not all practices have the same capacity to mobilise and valorise other social and political practices. In other words, Gramsci is not an indifferent liberal pluralist.

A hegemonic apparatus, or a unity in translation of different hegemonic apparatuses, does indeed have a structure. However, the fundamental question for Gramsci is how such a structure of hegemonic apparatuses is constituted, because this determines the type of structure that it will become. Herein lies one of the real novelties of Gramsci's conceptualisation of the nature of modern social formations and of the formation of an adequate instrument of political leadership, or of a revolutionary political party.

Gramsci was not interested in the very widespread conception – dominant in his time, as diffused by neo-Kantianism – of a series of essentially unrelated value-spheres, a series of zones in society which are aggregated to form society but which are relatively, or sometimes even absolutely, autonomous from each other. He was aware that all social practices are interrelated, precisely because of his Marxist emphasis on social practices as social relations within a social totality, not merely as the expressions of some regional logics.

That led him to conceive of what I would describe as the "political constitution of the social". Politics, for Gramsci, was not conceived of as a moment of administration or command from above, but always in terms of the transformative dimensions of a social formation or relations between social formations. It is the transformative dimension, and the possibility of intervention by various projects, which then defines the possible concrete forms of "the social", or the social relations in which we live our everyday lives. Gramsci does not argue that politics emerges from and then separates itself from the social, as an administrative instance, in a process of rationalisation; such would be one of the readings of the political theory of a figure slightly older than Gramsci, namely, Max Weber. Rather, for Gramsci, politics figures as an immanent transformative instance of social relations that both go beyond it and also, in a certain sense, fall behind it.

This theory of what I have described as the "constitution of the political" leads Gramsci to conceive of the revolutionary political party not as the centre of this series of practices and relationships that are articulated in a hegemonic apparatus. He went beyond the conception of the party characteristic of classical German Social Democracy before the First World War. As I note in my book, however, Gramsci's notion of a political party, "the Modern Prince", remained in many ways a promise for the future, not realised in his time. In many respects, he outlined in the *Prison Notebooks* a novel theory of the political party that goes beyond the main currents of his own time, and indeed, also beyond his own prior practice in the "Bolshevisation" of the Italian Communist Party.

It has sometimes been assumed that "the "Modern Prince" in Gramsci is merely a codeword or a euphemism for actually-existing political parties in his own time. But that reading neglects the fact that in the *Prison Notebooks* Gramsci engaged in a very intense self-critique of his own political role and of the different conceptions of a political party that he had affirmed in his years as an activist. Those ranged from a rejection of the political party-form through to some of the undesirable elements of "Bolshevisation" [in 1924-5] and, at some moments, it needs to be admitted, making too many concessions to bureaucratic deformations of the party-form in his own practical work.

Gramsci engages in intense self-critique of this in the *Prison Notebooks*, as of many elements of his previous work, and wants to conceive of a qualitatively new form of a political party which that will be adequate to respond to what he sees as the challenges of the time. When he refers to the party as the "Modern Prince", in an allusion to Machiavelli, he is attempting to think through the capacity for a unitary but plural conception of a revolutionary political party, which becomes itself a laboratory for experimentation in the forms of democratic political practice that it will be necessary to carry outside the party into the society as a whole.

That party for the Gramsci of the *Prison Notebooks* thus does not function as the centre, or the origin, of a hegemonic apparatus. It does not just begin from a core group of militants in one particular zone of society who progressively articulate and develop their networks, spreading out through society. Gramsci conceived of the Modern Prince as a new type of dialectical-pedagogical political and social relation capable of being translated into different contexts and then, just as crucially, of being retranslated backwards, enriched by the dialectical pedagogical exchange and interchange. We have at the end a vision of the Modern Prince not as a particular geographical location in the society, or even as a pre-existing element, but as the result of all of these relations, translations, and re-translations, as they are constituted in an ongoing process.

Gramsci conceived of the revolutionary political party, in its institutional form, more as a "result" which could then be used to describe, retroactively, an entire political process, but which does not precede or determine it in the sense of a traditionally linear relation of cause and effect. More accurately, we should say that the revolutionary political party is itself a political process, a new type of social and political relation capable of continuously drawing new elements into a dialogue which will not simply transform those external elements but also transform the Modern Prince itself as an active social relation.

"THE DECISIVE ELEMENT"

Yes, the revolutionary political party is not an already-finished thing, with a "finished programme" and so on, which then just radiates out and "colonises" other groups. Trotsky argues in 'Lessons of October' that even the revolutionary party best-prepared in advance will probably need to face internal crises and transform itself to succeed in revolutionary conditions. But surely the party is central. It is the organised body of activists who are systematically and collectively politically active in a continuous way, not just at high points; who, with a continuously-developed and sustained theoretical basis, most resist the "conceptions of the world mechanically imposed by the external environment" [21]; who best represent a concentrated power of political initiative. As Gramsci put it: "The decisive element in every situation is the permanently organised and long-prepared force which can be put into the field when it is judged that a situation is favourable (and it can be favourable only in so far as such a force exists, and is full of fighting spirit). Therefore the essential task is that of systematically and patiently ensuring that this force is formed, developed, and rendered ever more homogeneous, compact, and self-aware" [22]. Or again: "The protagonist of the new Prince could... only [be] the political party" [23]. (Emphasis added).

Again, the question is: what type of party? And further: how is this party formed?

Gramsci was well aware that, in the broader sense, there is nobody without a party, or nobody who is not in a certain way a "partisan", even if only in a practical state, of certain choices, values and interests they share with others in similar social positions. Similarly, he recognised very clearly in the politics of his own time that the structured political party played a decisive role in the organisation of its class's forces. Furthermore, he noted that there were important differences between the party organisation of different classes or social groups, differences that he argued needed to be analysed in terms of the social and economic relations that structured the social base of those parties.

However, when Gramsci attempts in prison to outline a theory of a new type of party, the "Modern Prince", I think he was attempting to move beyond any conception of political organisation that was instrumentalist, or that could be subjected to instrumentalist deformations. It is therefore not a case, it seems to me, of stating that, regardless of complicating and intervening factors, the party remains "central", in either the first or the last instance. This way of stating the problem presupposes precisely the element that Gramsci was attempting to problematise – namely, the process that constitutes and makes possible such a party, or if you like, "centre" of directly political coordination, organisation and leadership. Like Machiavelli, Gramsci recognised that the type of political formation that he wanted and that he thought would be necessary for a workers' revolution was not pre-given in any of the models he had experienced himself; it would need to be actively constructed, and that meant thinking seriously about its constitution, that is, the process of constructing it and the ongoing "maintenance work" necessary to make it endure as an "organisation of struggle".

By focusing on the Modern Prince as a dynamic social relation of democratic pedagogy, I think Gramsci was attempting to develop an active conception of the dynamism that would be necessary for the formation – and continuous re-formation, internal development and transformation – of a genuinely effective political party, as a representative political instance of much wider social relations. That is, he had an expansive conception of the types of social relations that should be viewed as making up the Modern Prince, in all its complexity. This was not to deny in any sense that at decisive moments, in relation to specific objectives and on specific terrains of the social formation, coordinated and concentrated action would be necessary to deal decisive blows against the bourgeois class project – Gramsci's reflections on military metaphors and their significance for political struggle point to his clear sense of the significance of this (just as it did for figures throughout the history of early social democracy, from Engels and Kautsky to Lenin and Trotsky, for whom such open struggle between constituted political forces was a real and present possibility). It was to emphasise, however, that such an instance of coordination and organisation would only become strong enough to perform its role in the struggle if it developed an awareness of the dynamic social relations that made it possible, and with which it needed to work if it was to provide an expansive rather than limiting conception of political leadership. Rather than conceiving of the party as a "centre", it might be better in this Gramscian perspective to think of such explicitly institutional-political coordinating and organising functions as the tip of the iceberg of the Modern Prince, the visible 10 % supported by the invisible 90% below the waterline.

MARXISM AND MASS MOVEMENT

What bearing does any of this have in a situation where there is class struggle but no "hegemonic apparatus" of the working class? There appears to be a sort of Catch-22 here. Gramsci seems to be saying that a Marxist world view cannot be developed without having a mass revolutionary working-class movement; but how can this mass revolutionary working-class movement develop without having at least some pioneer elements with some approximation of a Marxist world view?

Gramsci is operating in a period in which there are mass revolutionary parties of the working class already in existence, and indeed where there is an accepted social form called a working class with which and against which people identify. Our own times are very different. The very existence of mass political parties that could be characterised as "of the working class" has been placed in doubt, depending on how we understand the phrase "of the working class", as a relation of possession, or of identification and so forth. Even more importantly, for many people, including people on the left, the notion of the working class itself has been radically placed in question.

Obviously we can and should have extended discussions about the definition of the working class. In my view, we can very easily demonstrate that the working class, defined as those who engage in wage-labour as the principal source of their access to the means necessary for their continuing existence, in a wage-labour/ capital relation, is now much larger than ever before in world history. It is expanding exponentially, to the point that in some so-called advanced capitalist countries the percentage of the population that could be defined as the working-class in the broadest terms approaches 70 or 80%, if not more.

The difficulty, of course, is that many of the members of this working class in no sense identify subjectively with the working class, and have various other identifications which they may see as more important. I would suggest that at this stage in history the workers' movement in the broadest sense is confronted with the challenge of attempting to recompose notions of the working class and rethinking ways in which we can place the question of labour relations at the centre of social and political discussions.

Regardless of the other elements that exist in people's lives, which are certainly not unimportant, one element that all members of the broadly-defined working class have in common is the daily empirical fact of being subjected continously to a wage-labour/ capital relation. In other words, while we can be united by many things and often choose to unite with people for many different reasons, we are forced to share in common the fact of being exploited by capital (clearly, "exploitation" should be under-stood here in the sense in which Marx uses it, not as a moral category – at least, not in the first instance – but as a scientific category to describe the appropriation of surplus-value from wage-labour by owners of capital). We need to build new institutions that will be able to respond to that fact and transform those relations.

What does it mean to try to build a hegemonic apparatus in the con-temporary context? Against voices that declare the death of the working class, we need to insist that it is a possible project; but we also need to acknowledge, I think, that it is a project that will only be successful if it is able to acknowledge the very real difficulties and challenges it presently confronts. The attempt to construct a hegemonic apparatus of the workers' movement, and the plurality of different hegemonic practices that will be necessary to compose it, is in many respects a process that still needs to occur within the contemporary working class or working classes, conceived in a broader sense. Years of defeats, disaggregation and transformation of social relations and practices have severely damaged if not destroyed some of the older traditions and institutions that were identified as "of the working class", and helped to give a sense of the "unity in diversity" that the working class always was and is even more so today. We need to continue the struggle within the working class to build the institutions that can help to recompose a more composite social body, which will be capable of confronting the capitalist class in political terms; in the first and not the last instance, this includes political struggle itself, as an active form of aggregation, or drawing together of forces in struggle.

What does that mean concretely? I think it includes a wide series of cultural practices, of different ways of linking together practices that already exist with institutions of the working class. In the first place, this refers to institutions inside the trade-union movement and to different associations and committees, even including sporting associations, com-munity groupings and so forth. All those remain important areas that need to be explored and built in order to find some way of linking everyday practices that pose the question and perspective of labour as a central way we organise our lives together in society.

It also means assuming a political responsibility, of the positing of explicitly political elements. I think that occurs on two levels. One, in the current period, is the positing of questions of the theoretical perspectives that are necessary to recompose the workers' movement. In my view, that involves a revitalisation of Marxism, and its recovery from the long series of deformations to which Stalinism subjected it. We need today a flourishing of a Marxist theoretical culture that seriously and concretely explores forms of thought that can help us to build the type of "culture" – in the broadest sense, as Gramsci or Raymond Williams would understand that word – that can sustain political struggles at all levels, both theoretical and practical. Another is the level of political organisation and intervention in ongoing forms of political resistance. We need to link together the theoretical cultures and the political, interventionist cultures, or in Gramsci's terms, we need to find the relations of ongoing and reciprocal "translation" between them that will enable both to flourish. It is only through the linking of theory and what Marx referred to as "material force" that both of them will be transformed and begin to forge the necessary active conception of workers' self-emancipation.

"THE LAST LENIN"

In hindsight, Lenin's fairly fragmentary writings from late 1921 onwards show us a record of a heroic battle – considering how ill he was, and the very difficult circumstances – but also that he was very far from fully appreciating what was going on in the nascent Stalinist counter-revolution and having an answer to it. You referred to the struggle for literacy, but that was not an innovation of that period. The Red Army during the civil war probably spent more time teaching soldiers how to read than it did fighting. How far did Gramsci reflect further on the processes of Stalinisation which were already under way when he was in the Soviet Union in 1922-3?

Lenin's last articles and reflections are indeed limited – necessarily so, given the difficult conditions in which they were composed. There is no need to overblow either their intrinsic importance or Gramsci's reflections on them. The importance of emphasising the centrality of the "last Lenin's" legacy for the *Prison Notebooks*, however, is to acknowledge the explicitly political dimensions of Gramsci's theory of hegemony – something which has not always been done, particularly in some

Eurocommunist and later Post-Marxist interpretations.

In that last period, Lenin was confronting the problem of the working class as a leading group inside the workers' state. It was no longer simply a question of opposition, of rallying the forces to oppose Tsarism, but a problem "within" the new "non-State State". What were the forms of leadership in which the working class needed to engage in order to be successful in its own project, which is the abolition of exploitation and making possible the removal of oppressive social relations?

There are elements in Lenin's final writings – and just as crucially, his practice – that show an emphasis or a tendency, a direction or an orientation which it is necessary to take, but they are obviously only very rudimentary coordinates.

In the *Prison Notebooks*, Gramsci wanted to take up those rudimentary coordinates and to elaborate them into a prospective mapping of the forms of proletarian political practice. It was precisely because he saw the various deceptive forms in which bourgeois hegemony had been established and consolidated in the long 19th century that he wanted to think through the new types of democratic practice that the working class needed to engage in to build its own project of a "politics of truth".

From 1926 onwards, at the very latest, Gramsci was quite clear on the nature of what had emerged in the Soviet Union and the ongoing process of Stalinisation and bureaucratisation. He objected to it quite explicitly in political terms. In a famous letter of 14 October 1926 which Togliatti refused to deliver, he explicitly condemned the political inadequacy of the responses of the Russian leadership. He regarded the attempted bureaucratic manipulation and censorship of the minority position in the Russian party as a dishonest form of conducting political struggle, particularly inside the leadership of the only communist party that had successfully carried through a revolution and founded a workers' state.

This perspective deepened in very substantive terms when he was in prison. That caused huge conflict inside the prison with other members of the Italian Communist Party and effectively led to his isolation inside the prison and difficult reverberations as news of his position and what he had been saying reached the outside. There is currently underway, in Italy and elsewhere, extensive research into the details of Gramsci's relation with the Party, with the Soviet leadership and even inside his wife's family, on the basis of newly available archival material. It is perhaps still too early to reach any definitive judgements on Gramsci's position. Nevertheless, from the material that has already become available and the first studies, it seems quite clear that Gramsci's "heterodoxy" was much greater than has been thought in the past. Furthermore, it seems clear that his dissent from the direction of the international communist movement, particularly in relation to the politics of the "Third Period", was well known, and constituted a very complicated factor in his party, personal and even familial relations.

Moreover, from the evidence of the critical edition of the *Prison Notebooks*, at least, some things are already quite clear: a principled condemnation of all forms of bureaucratic manoeuvring as a political technique; an absolute opposition to the politics of the "Third Period" and its triumphalism (the line of "after them, us", as a response to fascism); and a profound disagreement with the culture that had developed in the Communist movement, of top-down leadership. Gramsci's emphasis became increasingly strong over the years. Inside the Modern Prince, he argues, disaggregation is necessary. Breakdown and conflict are necessary in order to build the Modern Prince. It is through what we should call explicitly factionalism, struggle, disagreement, open and organised disagreement, that the Modern Prince is able to build itself.

That is not because this open conflict of policies would then, on the model of a scientific experiment, be a way of testing different theses in order to find the one "true" one and then to eliminate false ones. Rather, it is because such disaggregation and conflict is the nature of modern social relations and of the different interests that subtend them. This approach became for Gramsci a way of drawing the dynamic conflictuality of modernity inside his proposed party-form itself, as a positive and productive dimension of proletarian organisation.

This distinction between Gramsci and the orthodoxy which became dominant not only in Russia but in the Communist movement as a whole shows that Gramsci, despite all his important disagreements with other members of the far left — with Trotsky and with the Left Opposition, and with Bordiga — nevertheless needs to be claimed as a member of the anti-Stalinist, Marxist tradition. His positions can be regarded as one of the principled perspectives that rejected the deformation of Marxism, united with those other currents – fittingly, given their common rejection of the silencing of comradely debate by the imposition of a bureaucratic orthodoxy from above – in their often quite significant substantive and analytical disagreements.

GRAMSCI AND STALINISM

In the early 1930s, a whole "Right-Communist" current — Brandler, Thalheimer, Lovestone, and so on, people who had looked to Bukharin before 1928-9 — criticised the "Third Period" policies and Stalin's bureaucratic methods, including inside the USSR, but without identifying the Stalinist bureaucracy as a socially-distinct ruling caste, class, or incipient class, as the left oppositionists did. Do you think that Gramsci developed a sharper criticism of Stalinism than the "Right Communists" did?

I think it would be exaggerating to claim that Gramsci had a developed theory of the internal class composition of the Stalinist USSR, such as we can find in the Left Opposition or other far left currents such as Bordiga or the council communists. He did not. His disagreement with Stalinism emerged from concrete disagreements about particular problems of political strategy, both in the Italian party and in the international movement, which he saw as deleterious for the building of the mass forces he correctly regarded as necessary for any chance to defeat fascism. He disagreed openly with the use of bureaucratic manoeuvres to silence opposition inside the Russian party. His rejection of the perspective of the third period was based upon an assessment of its likely disastrous effects on the international working class movement, dividing it and weakening it. Insofar as Gramsci developed a principled political critique of Stalinism as a strategic international perspective and bureaucratic deformation inside the Russian process, there are points of affinity with many currents of the far left critique of the degeneration of the Bolshevik revolution into Stalinist dictatorship – which is not to say that they were the same or that all were equally valid on all points. From our perspective today, it is important to note that Gramsci's political principles, and the analyses that followed from them, were fundamentally incompatible with a regime that sought to weaken proletarian democracy, on all levels.

Did Gramsci ever comment on the question of "socialism in one country"?

Gramsci commented obliquely on that theme at a number of points in the *Prison Notebooks*. His insistence was always that the national and the international remain intertwined. Gramsci critically took up analyses of imperialism, and was concerned to a much greater extent than I think is acknowledged in many English-language commentaries with the dynamics of capitalist accumulation on an international scale.

The notion that "socialism in one country" could be a goal for the socialist movement, or even a possibility, must, I think, be acknowledged as incompatible with Gramsci's analysis of the necessary international dimensions of the capitalist mode of production, and thus the necessity for any attempts to negate it and replace it with socialism also to be international.

In this sense, Gramsci's perspective remained close to the early years of the Third International, when the "Russian question" was always analysed in relation to the international situation and the future of the Soviets was seen as fundamentally tied to the future of the international revolutionary movement.

In writings of the mid-1920s, like the Lyons Theses of January 1926, Gramsci wrote about seeking an economy "better fitted to the structure and resources of the country" for Italy...

First, the Lyons Theses were at a relatively earlier stage in Gramsci's development. I don't think there is any political opposition between Gramsci before prison, and Gramsci in prison, but I do think it is important to draw distinctions between the different periods. There is no "totalised" picture that is available from any one citation of Gramsci. It is necessary to put together all the perspectives and the general theory that is used to analyse them, paying close attention to the development of Gramsci's thought within and across the different political conjunctures.

Second, in relation to the "Bolshevisation" of the Italian party in 1924-5 and related political perspectives from this period, Gramsci made what I regard as errors, and what I think he came to regard as errors too, albeit ones that occurred in very difficult circumstances.

We should also note that not all the Lyons Theses were written by Gramsci. A full translation of all the theses into English with scholarly apparatus is currently underway. Clearly, an adequate comprehension of their significance, both in terms of Gramsci's development and that of the Italian Communist Party, can only be gained if we analyse them in the political context of their time and place.

Finally, the strategic perspective of Gramsci's contribution to the Lyons Theses should be noted: in many respects, they were an attempt to give a concrete response to Lenin's demand for western communists to devise revolutionary strategies and programmes based upon an accurate investigation of the class composition, balance of forces and real potentials for revolutionary transformation in their own societies. As Gramsci always acknowledged, any hegemonic project would need to be based upon a capacity to address fundamental problems of economic organisation, and to propose solutions to the problems that the bourgeoisie was structurally incapable of addressing.

EAST AND WEST

Italy and Russia in the early years of the 20th century are generally seen as Italy being part of "the West", and Russia of "the East". But in overall industrialisation they were not very far apart. In terms of the productivity of agriculture they were not very far apart.

The big specific difference was that Italy had a much larger urban proportion of the population. It had a much larger urban non-proletarian population. One of Trotsky's chief arguments in Results and Prospects *had been that Russia was exceptional in the smallness of the urban petty-bourgeoisie.*

Gramsci made implicit references to that difference of class structure between Italy and Russia, scattered through his writings, but I know of nowhere where he poses it squarely and tries to tease through the differences.

In my book I say that there has been too much emphasis placed on a few words cruelly ripped from their context in which Gramsci counterposes East and West. Gramsci's words are often not interpreted in terms of the debates of his time, where differences between "East" and "West" were also a major concern for other Marxists, above all Trotsky and Lenin.

The distinction between "East" and "West" was not peculiar to Gramsci, or even to Gramsci, Trotsky, and Lenin. It is an old theme that goes back a long way in Western political thought, as far back as the ancient Greeks and distinctions in Greek political thought between the (largely) Eastern "barbarians" and the civilised Greeks. The theme traverses the entire history of Western political thought and was also very present in the discussions of early Social Democracy. Kautsky's profound objections to the Russian Revolution were due, in part, to his different understanding of historical development, but also, in part to his conviction that there were "immature" political forms present in Russia, which made a successful socialist transition impossible.

Gramsci complexified this picture entirely, and was interested in conceiving the ways in which there are differences between social formations, but which are united in one international system.

Yes, Italy was much closer to Russia in decisive respects than it was to the United States or to England. In both Russia and Italy you had a relatively highly politicised working class in urban centres being a minority in social formations dominated by a massive peasantry. That is one reason why the Russian discussions on hegemony resonated with Gramsci so strongly, because he could see the links with his own situation.

And then even if we move to the most "Western" of all "Western" social formations, the United States, in Gramsci's analysis you see some very "Eastern" features. In the "East", Gramsci wrote, the political super-structures were less developed. That comment has often been taken out of context. I think Gramsci's analysis was that it had been easier, because of the relative lack of mediating institutions, to topple the Tsarist state, but the problem of construction after the revolution was much more difficult than it might have been in the western countries. That point was not one original to Gramsci; it was one he took quite directly from Lenin and Trotsky and the early debates of the Third International.

When Gramsci analyses the United States, he sees, with the emergence of "Fordism", something very similar to the pattern in Russia – a lack of mediating institutions that had been organically unified into a hegemonic apparatus. Even in the most "Western" of all "Western" social formations, you had elements that would seem not to correspond to the model of the sophisticated, elaborate, politicised civil society supposedly characteristic of the "West".

One of Gramsci's most important analytical developments in the *Prison Notebooks* was precisely to problematise the East-West dichotomy, and instead to concentrate much more strongly on the social relations inside different state forms.

PASSIVE REVOLUTION

There are some passages in which you describe "passive revolution" as "permanent structural adjustment avant la lettre", i.e. as relevant to recent times, and others where you protest against "a dominant interpretation that extends passive revolution to the contemporary world".

I use the term "permanent structural adjustment avant la lettre" simply as a rhetorical device to draw the reader's attention to some similarities and parallels – but also differences – with our own times. It is important to acknowledge the context in which Gramsci developed the concept of passive revolution.

He took it from Vincenzo Cuoco, who essayed the concept in the context of a discussion of the Neapolitan revolution. Gramsci used it first to analyse the Risorgimento, and then extended it in different ways and at different dates to consider states like Italy and Germany in comparison to France as a type of model of modern state formation.

Thirdly, he extended it out to cover an entire period of historical development, such that "passive revolution" might be read as coinciding with the epoch of imperialism, if not predating it.

Why did he do that? We need to remember that he developed these reflections in the 1930s. They were used as a counterpoint to the triumphalism of the Stalinist Third Period and its type of teleology, which saw a continuous accumulation of the "progress" of the revolutionary movement. In some ways Gramsci was close to Walter Benjamin's critique of the implicit idealism of German Social Democracy's concept of historical progress, from which Stalinism was not, in the last analysis, as distant as it claimed, with the thesis of "social fascism".

Gramsci was looking for a concept that could help him to explain the way in which things continued to "go on as they were", to use Benjamin's terms. Indeed, he came to see such stabilisation or at least maintenance of the established order despite deep conflicts and contradictions at social and political levels as the real crisis to which the revolutionary movement needed to respond. He was trying to develop a concept that would help him understand where he was, in the 1930s, and which would be a powerful enough narrative – analytically, historically and politically – to be able to be set against the dominant Stalinist one. While doing so, he was always very careful continually to refer to Marx's critique of political economy as his fundamental touchstone, seeking to measure the political significance of this new category with Marx's reflections on the nature and specificity of a mode of production, its specific social relations, the interaction of forces of production and so forth.

I wouldn't deny that the concept of passive revolution can have a more general analytical validity, and could indeed even be used to analyse processes up to the present day. Some contemporary scholars have been doing just that, with some interesting perspectives produced by such an optic, such as in the work of Adam Morton. But I think there are other concepts in Gramsci that demand equal attention for describing the present, as potentially more fruitful for our own situation.

For example, I think neo-liberalism might be more usefully described with the Gramscian category of a counter-reform. This has been emphasised by the Brazilian Gramscian Coutinho. With the concept of counter-reform, Gramsci is much more interested in juridical processes and the destruction of political forms solidified in the state which different classes had been able to access and use for their own ends. In neo-liberalism, the state has been used to dismantle itself, in a certain sense, at least at its social level, by different impositions which have made forms of class organisation even more difficult for the labouring and subaltern classes.

Using the concept of passive revolution today, I think, involves a gambit. We then have to develop an analysis that connects Gramsci's analysis through to our own, through continuities or transformations in the mode of production and in the political forces.

In all Gramsci's discussions of passive revolution, he was concerned with the presence of at least two elements, which set it apart from similar concepts in the Marxist tradition that have been used to characterise periods and forms of reaction or defeat of popular forces. Passive revolution is not simply Bonapartism. It is not simply revolution from above. It is not simply counter-revolution. It is a more complex category. In one sense, it is still a "revolutionary" process, or an overthrowing of the old and institution of new social forms. In a passive revolution, concrete gains are made in productivity or efficiency, political institutions are "modernised", and so forth. But it involves a pacifying element, whereby such "modernisation" is accompanied not, as in instances such as the French Revolution, with the large masses of the working classes becoming politically active, but on the contrary, with their deliberate and structural pacification by political means. Gramsci described this process as a molecular transformation, as a decapitation of mediating instances, the absorption of elements of the leadership of the popular classes into the state apparatus or into the hegemonic apparatus of the bourgeoisie. The masses are still indeed called to participate in a process of modernisation, but in a passive form, without being able to develop political forms such as had occurred in "non-passive revolutions", above all, the French. They are not allowed to make the transition from the economic-corporative to the political moment which would be the construction of their own hegemonic apparatus.

If we want to extend the Gramscian concept of "passive revolution" in its specificity and complexity to the contemporary situation, we first need to determine if both of these elements are present in it: both "revolution", of a type, and its passive deformation. In the neo-liberal programme of the last 30-35 years we can see the denial of political forms to the subaltern classes and the decapitation, co-option, subsumption of their representatives.

But as to the possibility of this process producing genuine qualitative and quantitative progress, in the form of some type of progress that could be reconciled with a narrative of modernisation, I think we have to be more sceptical. The neo-liberal programme has led to regression in many countries, most notably in some of the supposedly advanced capitalist states. It has led to a state in which there has been, not a "second modernity", as some social theorists suppose, but processes of de-modernisation, of the destruction of social forms, of a continual destruction, if not of productivity itself, at least of its possibility of social utilisation and distribution.

In sum, the notion of passive revolution can help to add new dimensions to an analysis of new forms of imperialism, but it needs to be used critically and with an attention to its historical embeddedness. As I have suggested, I think it may turn out, upon further reflection, that some of Gramsci's other categories have a greater critical purchase on the present.

A further point that I think is worth emphasising, against some interpretations of the notion of passive revolution, is that Gramsci was not Weber. Passive revolution does not denote some inevitable process of rationalisation which terminates in an iron cage. Gramsci was much more open and alert to the possibilities of struggle within passive revolution. It was precisely for this reason that he set out to develop the concept, against the fatalism of the Third Period perspective, which could legitimately be described as a philosophy of history with a Stalinist face.

Gramsci wrote at an advanced stage of his research and development of this concept that we need to link the concept of passive revolution quite directly with perspectives from Marx regarding the nature of the mode of production and the capacity of social formations for immanent transformation; but that we also need to purge Marx's perspectives of any trace of fatalism, which he admitted could be found in some prominent interpretations of Marx and possibly in Marx's ambiguities themselves. Gramsci always insisted that nothing is inevitable in these historical processes. They always depend on a political intervention, and are open to political transformation.

FUSION OF PHILOSOPHY WITH POLITICS? THE "DEMOCRATIC PHILOSOPHER"

Does Gramsci overstate the democratic and class character of philosophy when he writes of the fusion of philosophy with politics? He seems to posit a very close relation between Marxist philosophy, as he sees it, and a mass revolutionary working-class movement. That takes us back to a Catch-22: no Marxist philosophy without a mass revolutionary working-class movement, and no revolutionary mass working-class movement without Marxist philosophy. Yet many of the texts from Marx which Gramsci based himself on were written in the absence of any mass revolutionary working-class movement.

The notion of the "philosophy of praxis" in Gramsci has often been taken to be simply a euphemism for Marxism. The contention in my book, following a number of other Gramscian scholars, is that Gramsci used this term to describe a new philosophical position which represents his intervention into debates following the Russian Revolution about the nature of Marxism as both a philosophy and broader conceptions of the world. Gramsci's "philosophy of praxis" is therefore not simply equivalent with Marxism (which of course is never singular, but has always been defined in different ways by different political currents and perspectives); rather, it represents Gramsci's particular version of Marxism, or more precisely, his proposal for the further development of the Marxist tradition that he inherited. Furthermore, it was not only a proposal regarding what a Marxist philosophy could be, but also included a critical perspective on the political nature of philosophy as such, even in its seemingly least "political" forms.

In his analysis of previous philosophies, Gramsci identified various contradictions at work in them, whether they were idealist or materialist. He came to a position that argued that in so far as they involved various forms of linguistic practice, that is, complex forms of social relations, philosophical statements were already political instances — "political" here meaning the transformative instance of social relations and practices. Already, in a sense, philosophical statements serve to organise human social relations — linguistic and conceptual relations that form an integral part of all other social relations, overdetermining them and overdetermined by them in their turn.

Gramsci argued that previous philosophies, even those that might at first sight seem to be at a far remove from explicitly political themes and focused instead on classically "speculative" notions, had been engaged in highly mediated but nevertheless political forms of organisation, of the shaping, crafting, and transformation of conceptions of the world.

He therefore wanted to investigate what could be a philosophical form that would be adequate to the goals and practices of a democratic workers' movement. He came to the view that it is only by acknowledging the always-already-practical nature of philosophy that it is possible not only to criticise previous forms of philosophy (including, crucially, the criticism of previous conceptions of Marxist philosophy), but also to go further and attempt to develop a new form of philosophical practice that would arguably be more genuinely philosophical than the contending and rival positions, if we are to understand philosophy as always a practice, as a "love of wisdom", in the classic sense.

The claim would be not to be the "wise man" (the sophos of presocratic philosophy), but simply to be a lover of wisdom; that is, not the claim to already possess the truth in some form, but to be searching for it. The Western philosophical tradition in fact begins precisely from such a "distance taken", from the claim to possess truth already in the form of an achieved wisdom, to the claim that we are merely seeking truth, or trying to become wise. For Gramsci, that conception of the search for wisdom, and of being open to the continual corrections of history, became a way of fusing history and philosophy. Philosophy became a historical practice. It also became political, insofar as philosophy, as one of the most developed forms of conceptual-linguistic organisation, can be seen as one of the forms in which a conception of the world is created and crafted – a political relation of leadership.

Gramsci wanted to pose the question of the interaction between politics, in this much broader sense, and philosophy in the workers' movement. Ultimately, Gramsci came to the position that the politician was a philosopher, and the philosopher was a politician, at various degrees of mediation. The philosopher was already engaged in the political practice of comprehending the transformation of social relations, intervening in those transformations by means of organising and socialising, via linguistic and conceptual practice, their potential theoretical significance. The politician was also engaged in a comprehension, or a grasping, of philosophical problems. Why? Because philosophy, according to this perspective, could not be defined in its totality as simply concepts and ideas, but was always constituted as a shared, social conception of the world that actively worked to organise it, a particular mode of coherent organisation.

In this perspective Gramsci's reference once again was to his great "master" — in a classical sense, the person from whom he learned, and whose teaching enabled him to speak for himself — that is, Lenin. Gramsci argues quite specifically that in elaborating a hegemonic apparatus of the working class, equipping the Russian working class with the institutions and the perspectives that would be necessary for self-government, Lenin accomplished not only a political act but also a philosophical event of great importance.

"The theoretical-practical principle of hegemony has also epistemological significance, and it is here that Ilyich [Lenin]'s greatest theoretical contribution to the philosophy of praxis should be sought. In these terms one could say that Ilyich advanced philosophy as philosophy in so far as he advanced political doctrine and practice. The realisation of a hegemonic apparatus, in so far as it creates a new ideological terrain, determines a reform of consciousness and of methods of knowledge: it is a fact of knowledge, a philosophical fact..."

Reforming the institutions in which we live socially also reforms our conceptions of the world. It changes the foundation of philosophy, providing the possibility for a new conception of the world and therefore for the development of new forms of philosophy.

In order to specify the nature of this type of philosophical practice, Gramsci developed the figure of the "democratic philosopher". He mentions this concept only once in the *Prison Notebooks*, but in many respects it can be taken as his proposal for a new type of intellectual and new type of philosopher, as an integral element of a broader political movement: "a new type of philosopher, whom we could call a 'democratic philosopher' in the sense that he is a philosopher convinced that his personality is not limited to himself as a physical individual but is an active social relationship of modification of the cultural environment".

In that figure there was, I think, a conception of a new form of philosopher that would be adequate to democratic political forms. The previous, aristocratic, conception of the philosopher as the speculative metaphysician standing above society – or, as Nietzsche claimed, thinking thousands of miles above others — that conception was fundamentally negated by Gramsci. He was conceiving of the way in which, following Marx in the Theses on Feuerbach, the "educator" was also "educated". That is, philosophers – whether "professional" philosophers or "everyday" philosophers, remembering that for Gramsci we are all philosophers in some sense, in so far as we try to think coherently about the world and our place in it – were already necessarily involved in different social relations that had formed them and that provided not only the basic linguistic conceptuality they used in order to elaborate their thoughts, at different levels of coherence, but also all the problems they considered in their philosophical practice. The question then was whether someone could acknowledge the way in which they were continually interpellated, continually called into different relations and forced to respond to them in the form of a dialogue. The "democratic philosopher", for Gramsci, became the philosopher who was mature enough to acknowledge the foundation of their thought in the common everyday practices of the people, a philosopher who was open to the capacity for transformation of those instances, and sought himself or herself to contribute to their transformation through his or her intervention in linguistic, conceptual, or political forms.

Ultimately, Gramsci's figure of the "democratic philosopher" is not simply the philosopher in the traditional sense at all, but comes to be equated with, in Machiavelli's terms, the active citizen, engaged in acts of virtuous self-governance. We could say that, in Marxist terms, the democratic philosopher is an example of the type of everyday search for wisdom that is – and needs to become even more – an essential element of the ongoing self-emancipation of the working class and its struggle to enlarge the field of active democratic participation in the organisation of society.

The revolutionary socialist as democratic philosopher

Martin Thomas discusses *The Gramscian Moment*

ANTONIO GRAMSCI WAS an Italian Marxist, a founding member of the Italian Communist Party in its revolutionary period of the 1920s, and chief leader of the CP from late 1923 to 1926.

Jailed by Mussolini's fascist regime from 1926 until shortly before his death in 1937, Gramsci wrote his *Prison Notebooks* which have gradually become, as Peter Thomas notes, "a classic of twentieth-century social theory".

The *Notebooks* were first published in Italy in 1948-51, by an Italian Communist Party which by then was thoroughly Stalinist. It used them to back up its "national-popular" (reformist, class-collaborationist) strategy. The *Notebooks* were, after all, notebooks, not texts finished for publication. And, since Gramsci became very ill in prison, and often had to break off writing, they are mostly fragmentary.

That made them cryptic enough for the Communist Party to exploit them. From early on, dissidents criticised the Communist Party's interpretation and argued that Gramsci should properly be read as a revolutionary working-class socialist who never abandoned his principles of the early 1920s.

The influence of the *Notebooks* spread gradually. A selection was translated into English in 1971 (the Further Selections, published in 1995, and the complete translation being done by Joseph Buttigieg, are still difficult to obtain). Translations into French were published from 1978 onwards (with a compact volume of selections edited by André Tosel coming out in 1983); translations into German, from 1991.

Today, in Peter Thomas's words, Gramsci's *Notebooks* are "a significant point of reference in such diverse fields as history, sociology, anthropology, literary studies, international relations, and political theory". In the universities, Gramsci is referred to more than any other Marxist writer, maybe even more than Marx himself. Students in any one of a wide range of courses of study will come across Gramsci even if they come across no other Marxist writer.

That is partly because there are now many more "Gramscis" than the old Communist Party "Gramsci" and the revolutionary Marxists' "Gramsci". A whole school of writers, mostly moving on from some background in or around the old Communist Parties, have made of Gramsci a bridge from socialist concerns to varieties of "post-Marxism" (in politics, varieties of liberalism), more or less imbued with post-modernism.

Gramsci's best-known concept, "hegemony", has been amputated from its basis in working-class politics, and turned into a puff-word for all manner of nondescript alliances.

Peter Thomas has written a book about Gramsci that both understands his thought as based in the great mass revolutionary socialist workers' movement that flowered briefly between the Russian Revolution of 1917 and the triumph of Stalinism, and explores his originality. The book both covers well-trampled ground (hundreds of articles and books about Gramsci now appear every year), and traverses it in a new direction (no other comprehensive book on Gramsci has approached the *Prison Notebooks* from the same angle).

It is well worth the effort of reading. It is an effort. Though Peter Thomas can write well, on the whole the book bears the marks of its origins in a PhD thesis. When working on *Capital*, Marx wrote to Engels that he was "expanding" the book "since those German scoundrels estimate the value of a book in terms of its cubic capacity". The PhD mill of today's universities seems to estimate value in terms of volume of references and footnotes.

Thus the book starts not with Gramsci, but with a discussion of the old French Communist Party philosopher Louis Althusser and his criticism of Gramsci. Less respectful of Althusser than Peter Thomas is, I see this starting point as like trying to get a first overview of an inspiring building by crawling into it through its drains.

Moreover, even if one were more respectful of Althusser, his critique of Gramsci is only a few pages in his book *Reading Capital*, and in them "Gramsci" functions more as a straw man for Althusser's own concerns than as a real figure.

Peter Thomas's next approach is through a side-door: a discussion of Perry Anderson's critical essay of 1976, *The Antinomies of Antonio Gramsci* (New Left Review I/100). Critique of Anderson is the headline feature of chapter two, and a major organising theme of much of the first half of the book. The obliquity of approach is still unfortunate, but not because Anderson's essay is of little worth. On the contrary: despite reading and re-reading Peter Thomas's chapters, I still think Anderson's essay is sharp and illuminating, and that Thomas has shown no more than minor errors.

From about chapter five, Peter Thomas gets into his stride. He demystifies the concept of "hegemony" in Gramsci, from which so many speculations are spun, showing that it meant nothing other than working-class political leadership, achieved through sound use of united-front tactics. He defines united front tactics as "the final strategic advice of Lenin to the Western working-class movement before his death", "the only possible foundation for a realistic and responsible socialist politics" — and radically different from "the nationalist and non-class-based perspective of a 'popular front'," i.e. the sort of strategic alliance with bourgeois forces enforced by the Stalinist parties in the 1930s. He shows that Gramsci was won over to united-front tactics by Trotsky while he was in Russia in 1922-3, and further that Gramsci's views were deeply influenced by Lenin's efforts, in his last years, under the New Economic Policy, to find a sound political basis, free of the abruptnesses of "war communism", for an alliance between the Bolshevik leadership, the broader working class, and the USSR's peasant majority.

Gramsci's innovation, so Peter Thomas shows, was not the introduction of the concept "hegemony", but his ideas about building what Gramsci calls a working-class "hegemonic apparatus", which fights to win a working-class majority and working-class political power utilising the principles of the united front. "A class's hegemonic apparatus is the wide-ranging series of institutions and practices — from newspapers to educational organisations to political parties — by means of which a class and its allies engage their opponents in a struggle for political power"

[24].

Where Gramsci discusses "consent" and "coercion" as aspects of leadership, his social-reformist interpreters have presented "consent" and "coercion" as mutually-exclusive alternatives. They have then argued that modern capitalist rule rests very largely on "consent" and claimed therefore that all strategy must be directed at "consent". They conclude that winning wide "consent" by a sort of diffuse cultural coalition-building is what "hegemony" really means.

Peter Thomas point out that for Gramsci, "leadership [or, what for him was pretty much a synonym] hegemony and domination are [only] strategically differentiated forms of a unitary political power".. For the workers' party to win "consent" from the poorer classes is not an alternative to it mobilising class-struggle "coercion" against the wealthy classes. On the contrary: "A class's ability... to secure the consent of allies... also relies upon its ability to coordinate domination over the opponents of this alliance" [25].

Or again: "Without an attempt to transform leadership in civil society into a political hegemony or into the nascent forms of a new political society, civil hegemony itself will be disaggregated and subordinated to... the existing political hegemony of the ruling class" [26]. He succinctly defines Gramsci's concept of hegemony as "a Marxist theory of the constitution of the political" [27].

Peter Thomas takes up a phrase used (as he himself notes) only once by Gramsci, "the democratic philosopher", and convincingly makes it the fulcrum of the later chapters of his book. Gramsci argued that everyone is a "philosopher", the question only being how conscious and "coherent" the philosophy (the overview of the world and history) is. Peter Thomas discusses exactly what "coherent" means here.

He argues that Gramsci's famous term "philosophy of praxis" is not just a euphemism which he used in his *Prison Notebooks*, for fear of censorship, in place of writing bluntly "Marxism". Gramsci, he writes, offers a new conception of philosophy — "as a relationship of hegemony"; as a "conception of the world" developed in dialogue with the "senso comune" (roughly, common sense) of a definite social class.

The "democratic philosopher" is the purposeful, educating and self-educating, socialist activist. "The older 'form' of philosophy" is "superannuated" and must be "replaced by new practices of the socialist movement".

This is, so to speak, a democratic and republican conception of philosophy rather than the absolute-monarch conception of earlier ages, or the constitutional-monarch conception which arises when scientific development has quelled some of the pretensions of speculation.

Rather than having "philosophers" operating on a different plane from everyday people, who are left to the improvisations of "common sense", or using the constraints of mass "common sense" to censor the "philosophers" (as the Catholic Church does), the "dialectical pedagogy" of "the democratic philosopher as collectivity" seeks, in Gramsci's words, "to construct an intellectual-moral bloc that renders politically possible a mass intellectual progress and not only a progress of small intellectual groups".

The "intellectuals" — of worker or of better-off background — must be "permanently active persuaders" in the mass movement, operating "in a reciprocal relationship of 'democratic pedagogy' in which those 'intellectuals'... are at least as often 'the educated' as 'the educators'."

It is "a project of democratic expansion" — "or, as Gramsci wrote in the depths of [Stalin's] Third Period [1928-34], 'in politics of the masses, to say the truth is a political necessity, precisely'." [28]

In some passages of the *Prison Notebooks*, Gramsci writes as if there is an absolute unity of theoretical understanding and practical activity — as if "philosophical" perception is impossible without being "an historical, political achievement of a [whole] class" engaged in actively changing the world [29].

"Unity of theory and practice" is often said to be a Marxian idea. But, as Peter Thomas points out, it is much older than Marx; and, as he does not point out, the phrase was nowhere used by Marx.

I do not know when the phrase was lifted from older writers (such as Hegel) and dropped into Marxist discourse. George Lukacs used it a lot, but I doubt he was the first. It became a "conventional wisdom" with Stalinism.

The phrase "unity of theory and practice" is often interpreted as meaning such things as that practice should be guided by theory and theory should be translated into and tested by practice, which are indeed good sense; and so it has usually been accepted by anti-Stalinist Marxists.

But "unity of theory of practice" is a bad way of expressing that good sense. The necessary and proper linkage of theory and practice does not merge them into a single unity. They remain distinct. Practice will always be richer and more complex than theory; theory will always run ahead of practice, to some degree or another. Much theory has only a very distant relation to "practice" in the sense of political activity. Disunity of theory and practice — that is, scope for "provisional thinking", autonomous from immediate practical imperatives — is necessary for intellectual progress.

As Theodor Adorno, refusing to knuckle under to Stalinism, wrote: "The call for a unity of theory and practice has increasingly demoted theory to the status of handmaiden... The practical identifying mark that was being demanded of all theory has also became a stamp of censorship... Theory... became a part of the very politics from which it was intended to find a way out" [30].

The catchcry "unity of theory and practice" has had malign effects in the anti-Stalinist left too. The idea that any theoretical dissent is idle chatter unless it can show quick practical conclusions has stifled thought; so has the habit of quickly shutting off any unfamiliar thought by "tagging" it with an uncongenial practical conclusion. ("If you say that the Stalinist states were worse for the working class than ordinary capitalism, then you end up backing US foreign policy" — that sort of argument).

Gramsci accepted the formula "unity of theory and practice", and even sharpened it to "identity of theory and practice". It is not clear, but it seems that he conceived of this identity as belonging to a "modern Prince", a "hegemonic apparatus", which "remained no more than a proposal for the future, not a concrete reality, in his time — or in our own" (Peter Thomas's words [31]).

What, then, can be done in actual time, Gramsci's or our own? Gramsci, I think, saw his "proposal for the future" as not something to be waited for, but something to be worked for, starting now. The sharpening of the formula "unity of theory and practice" to "identity of theory and practice" indicates that, even if you think it possible, it cannot be a precondition for action, but rather something to be worked towards.

"The most important observation to be made about any concrete analysis of the relations of force is the following: that such analyses cannot and must not be ends in themselves (unless the intention is merely to write a chapter of past history), but acquire significance only if they serve to justify a particular practical activity, or initiative of will. They reveal the points of least resistance, at which the force of will can be most fruitfully applied; they suggest immediate tactical operations; they indicate how a campaign of political agitation may best be launched, what language will best be understood by the masses, etc.

"The decisive element in every situation is the permanently organised and long-prepared force which can be put into the field when it is judged that a situation is favourable (and it can be favourable only in so far as such a force exists, and is full of fighting spirit). Therefore the essential task is that of systematically and patiently ensuring that this force is formed, developed, and rendered ever more homogeneous, compact, and self-aware..." [22]

"The protagonist of the new Prince could... only [be] the political party" [23].

The process of assembling and preparing the party starts long before it can become a decisive mass movement and, by the richness of its theory and the power of its practice, come close to at least a metaphorical sort of "unity of theory and practice". Gramsci analysed three elements required to form a party — mass membership, "principal cohesive element", and intermediate cadres. He wrote of the second element, "numerically weak", that it cannot "form the party alone", but "it could do so" — i.e. make a start at forming a party — "more than could the first element" [32]. And, by obvious implication, it should do so. It should assemble a nucleus even before a mass membership is possible; and without such a nucleus, developed in advance, mass membership alone cannot form a party.

Gramsci's arguments point to starting the work of party-building now, even if only on a small and primitive scale.

The question of the revolutionary working-class party is strangely marginalised in Peter Thomas's book (there is not even an index entry for "party"). It is as if accepting the "identity of theory and practice" as the true shape of a "hegemonic apparatus" of the working class leads to concluding that when that full "identity" (or anything that could metaphorically be called that) is impossible, no lesser linkage of theory and practice is much worth bothering with.

Near the end of the dissertation on which this book is based, Peter Thomas says of Gramsci: "His insights into the forms of a possible proletarian hegemony retain today their fertility for further theoretical and practical investigation, awaiting the energies and initiatives of a reviving working-class movement which alone will be able to confirm and, if necessary, to transform them in practice".

Insights are not things that can "await". Or is it the people who have the "insights" who should "await"? Until they can be mobilised by "energies and initiatives of a reviving working-class movement"? In that scheme, instead of the "intellectuals" (of worker and other origin) providing "initiative", it is the job of the generally relatively passive mass to do that.

Peter Thomas brings an array of talents to this book. He came into radical politics at the University of Queensland, in Australia, where he studied from 1992 to 2000. The first name mentioned in the acknowledgements in the book, and rightly so, is that of Dan O'Neill, his teacher in the English department at UQ, a veteran of the Brisbane left, and still active today after retirement from the university.

From Dan, I think we can say at a minimum, Peter Thomas got a scrupulousness about texts, a respect for the classics, a breadth of inquiry, and, in short, a fundamental opposition to all the shoddinesses of postmodernism. Though never joining a Trotskyist group, Peter Thomas worked closely in campaigns and study groups with Trotskyists such as Murray Kane, Melissa White, and myself: he was surely, by the time he left Brisbane, a Trotskyist of some sort.

With remarkable energy, he got a series of grants enabling him to study in Berlin, in Naples, in Rome, and in Amsterdam. Much unlike the ordinary run of English-speaking academics, he writes with a fluent command of the literature, and a first-hand knowledge of the debates, in Italian and German as well as English. I can't help but think that there have been downsides in the transition from political activist to cosmopolitan academic. The book is structured at odds with the dialogic conception of philosophy which it argues. Rather than engaging with the interactions, fruitful or botched, of the revolutionary Marxists with the "senso comune" (common sense) of the working class, it takes its markers from the debates in Marxist, post-Marxist, and Marxisant academia and within the old official Communist Parties, as if those constituted the universe of "Marxism", in abstraction from political practice.

The book remains recognisably Trotskyist. Fabio Frosini, the commentator on Gramsci who gets by far the greatest number of favourable references in the book, testifies to this when, in a generally warm review of it, he comments disapprovingly that he finds its discussion of Gramsci's affinity to Trotsky and hostility to Stalinism the least convincing element.

Despite all criticisms, this is a rich and valuable text, a source of many more ideas than can be mentioned in a short review.

Anderson's antinomies

By Martin Thomas

PETER THOMAS'S BOOK *The Gramscian Moment* gives over its second chapter to a discussion and critique of Perry Anderson's study from 1976, *The Antinomies of Antonio Gramsci* (New Left Review I/100). Large parts of later chapters are also polemic against Anderson. I am still not convinced that the polemic against Anderson is just and well-directed.

When Anderson wrote, the "Eurocommunists" were on the rise in the Communist Parties of Western Europe. They argued that Gramsci's writings showed a "third way" for socialist strategy, beyond traditional Stalinism (which they more or less equated with Leninism) and traditional reformism. In fact, "Eurocommunism" would become an ideological device for shifting the CPs into only cosmetically-modified social-democratic policies, and shifting many CPers into plain bourgeois liberalism. That was not so clear at the time.

In 1976 Anderson himself was at his closest to (the Mandelite strand of) Trotskyism, as he showed in his book *Considerations on Western Marxism*, published that same year. He had moved to that political stance from an earlier position, before 1968, closer to a sort of left social democracy, and codified in an article, "Problems of Socialist Strategy" (in the collection *Towards Socialism*), which drew heavily on Gramsci. The 1976 article was a Trotskisant critique both of Anderson's own earlier views (he was explicit about the self-criticism), and of the Eurocommunists' use of Gramsci.

Peter Thomas would agree with the 1976 Anderson's arguments against what the Eurocommunists or the young Perry Anderson constructed from passages of Gramsci. Probably (we can't know) the Trotskisant Anderson of 1976 would not have disagreed with the political ideas implied in what Thomas argues is the main drift of Gramsci's notebooks if read carefully and loyally.

The scope of the disagreement between Anderson and Thomas is thus limited. A large part of it comes down to Anderson saying: there are slippages, ambiguities, and discrepancies in Gramsci's notebooks, which have been seized on by people like the Eurocommunists. And Thomas responding: if you take passages in context, and pay due attention to the development of Gramsci's thought rather than stopping at particular formulations, then there really is no such sizeable slippage and ambiguity.

Anderson sets a frame, and limits, to his critique of Gramsci's notebooks, by pointing out that Gramsci's arguments about "hegemony", "war of position", and so on were formulated in reaction to and polemic against the "Third Period" turn of the Stalinists (p.11, p.60). Gramsci had never and could never have intended them as a repudiation of revolutionary perspectives and a shift towards what Thomas aptly calls a "cultural syndicalism", a reduction of socialist activism to a gradual process of winning cultural influence in one sphere of society after another.

They also pointed us towards important questions about what extra elements revolutionary socialist strategy needed in order to deal with the facts of long-lasting, well-rooted bourgeois democracy in many West European countries, conditions different from Russia in 1917.

However, in the fragmentary and unfinished text of Gramsci's *Prison Notebooks*, argued Anderson, there was repeated "slippage" of concepts, a pattern of discrepancies and "antinomies", which had given false authority to the vagaries of both the Eurocommunists and Anderson's earlier self.

In several passages Gramsci had drawn a contrast between "West" and "East" in which the "West" was characterised by a State well-developed in its relationship with, or even subsuming, civil society, as contrasted with a State that was relatively brittle because less integrated with networks in society, and more reduced to a detached apparatus of repression.

From that contrast in structures, Gramsci had deduced a contrast of strategy. Strategy in the "West" must be based on "war of position", "civil hegemony", and "the united front", not "war of manoeuvre" as in the East. Further, Gramsci had used the concept of "hegemony" to analyse both bourgeois political power and working-class political power (in the USSR after 1917, or in other countries in the future), without clear indications of the differences involved. The tendency was to elide or blur over a number of issues:

• The question of revolutionary force; the fact that the bourgeoisie's ability to win "consent" even in the most bourgeois-democratic country depends on backstop state force, and that working-class power requires the use of force to break up and overcome that bourgeois state force [33];

• The radical difference between bourgeois revolutions, in which an already-powerful and already-privileged social class can manipulate plebeian foot-soldiers to win a future which none of them clearly foresee, but which evolves according to laws of capitalist market economics not under their control; and working-class revolutions, in which lucid and active political consciousness must be central [34];

• The difference between the sort of political manipulation, designed largely to organise passivity, through which the bourgeoisie wins "consent" for its rule, and the active revolutionary alliances in which the working class wins "consent" for its bid to take and hold power.

Inadvertently, Gramsci ended up reproducing some of the arguments which Karl Kautsky had used in 1911 when he rejected Rosa Luxemburg's call for the German socialist movement to actively discuss mass strikes, and boldly demand a republic in Germany, in favour of a more cautious, step-by-step strategy. Gramsci's "war of position" could in some passages reasonably be read as something like the "strategy of attrition" proposed by Kautsky, both of them being justified by the complexity and solidity of bourgeois rule in the "West" [35].

Although, so Anderson noted, Gramsci sometimes writes of "hegemony" as having to be a synthesis of coercion and consent, or as something operated by the State, the frequent drift is to see the terrain of hegemony as "civil society" rather than the State, or to blur any boundary between "civil society" and the State .

A blurring of the boundary between "civil society" and the State makes it "impossible and unnecessary to distinguish between bourgeois democracy and fascism" [36]. Oddly, though Gramsci himself "had no illusions about the significance of the innovations imposed by the counter-revolutionary dictatorship of which he was a victim", "in his Prison Writings there is no comprehensive comparison of bourgeois democracy and fascism" [37].

All that cannot but help along temptations, imposed anyway by the overawing effect of solid bourgeois power, to leave in vagueness those areas where working-class strategy must go beyond patient efforts to secure advantage, or less disadvantage, in the various areas of civil society.

A blurring of boundaries between "civil society" and the State was much used by Eurocommunist polemicists at that time in argument against the revolutionary left. The State, so those polemicists would argue, had spread itself and integrated itself with networks of civil society so much that the old Leninist talk of "smashing the bourgeois state" was simply outdated. Socialists had to work "in and against the state" to transform its institutions bit by bit.

Anderson recognised that there are "grey areas" between State and civil society [38]. But he argued against "Eurocommunist" blurring, and for remembering the critical role of the State's core function – "armed bodies of men" maintaining the monopoly of legitimate violence – in lynchpinning all "consent". He also, usefully, signalled that there are important modes of bourgeois domination in society which can be classified under neither "coercion" nor "consent". And he pointed out that the bourgeoisie's means for securing consent lie not only, and maybe not even mainly, in civil society. In bourgeois democracy, the parliamentary form of the state itself is a chief means of organising the working class as an atomised scattering of individuals and imbuing them with the illusion that they already have political self-determination.

Thomas agrees with Anderson's rejection of Eurocommunism and of the left social democratic politics of Anderson's past. However, he finds Anderson's reading of Gramsci "highly over-determined by the international political conjuncture… and not a little influenced by Anderson's reckoning of accounts with his own political and theoretical past" [39]. Anderson was reading the Eurocommunism into Gramsci. The "antinomies" were Anderson's own, not Gramsci's.

Thomas discounts some of the passages in which Gramsci polemicises against "permanent revolution", conflating it with ultra-leftism, as "overdetermined by Gramsci's personal antipathy for Trotsky". The antipathy, he says, was shaped by Gramsci's reaction to Trotsky's fierce (and eventually successful) berating of Gramsci around the time of the Fourth Congress of the Communist International in 1922 in order to shift Gramsci from his alliance with Bordiga and towards accepting the policy of the united front.

Thomas's first objection to Anderson's article is that it is not careful enough on textual details. Drawing on Gianni Francioni, Thomas argues that Anderson's portrayal of Gramsci's evolution through different characterisations of the relationship of the State to civil society is inaccurate, describing as late some formulations which in fact came early, and as early some formulations which actually came later [40].

"'Anderson's error', as Francioni demonstrated, 'consists precisely in believing that, in the diverse texts to which he refers, the notion of the State is the same'... However, as Francioni... argued, [with] the first emergence of the concept of the 'integral State' in... October 1930... 'the dialectical "identity-distinction between civil society and political society" produces an enlarged concept of the state in which the poles of such unity are included: they are 'the constitutive elements of the state in an organic and larger sense (state properly called and civil society)'... " [41]

L'Unità of 7 May 2007 includes an interview with Gianni Francioni in which Francioni describes how he sees Gramsci's "broad vision": as one "that shows us how the Bolshevik East was backward for him. Inadequate to serve as a model for politics and revolution in the West..."

L'Unità, although the strapline on its masthead still describes it as "founded by Antonio Gramsci in 1924", is now linked to the Democratic Party in Italy, the merger of a large right-wing chunk of the old Communist Party with a segment of the old Christian Democrats. It is surely naïve to take Francioni's dissection of details as only a search for precision, and as demolishing Anderson's whole argument rather than showing secondary flaws, without taking account of Francioni's political views. Anderson's core argument is not that Gramsci *moved towards* more confused formulations over time. It is that confused and unclarified formulations *exist* in the *Notebooks*.

Thomas argues that "the concept of the integral State" is Gramsci's real "novel contribution to Marxist political theory".

Before studying Thomas's argument on this point, consider a review in English of Peter Thomas's book, by Chris Nineham of the SWP splinter group Counterfire, which explicitly endorses Thomas's critique of Anderson. It shows how that critique can be read in a grievous way.

Nineham: "Anderson's view was that Gramsci works with conflicting descriptions of the relations between 'civil society', 'political society' and the 'state'. Through a close reading Peter Thomas shows that in fact the confusion was Anderson's. The state for Gramsci is the coercive element in class rule, political society the explicitly political process, while civil society includes apparently more neutral institutions. [Nineham has garbled it here. The "integral State", in Gramsci, is not just "the coercive element". Moreover, a few lines later Nineham will say that the state is the "apparently more neutral" element. But let it pass...] "Gramsci developed a sophisticated view of these three as separate 'moments' or aspects of the way the ruling class maintains its power, its 'hegemonic project'. Civil society, political society and the state are distinct but mutually reinforcing elements of the superstructure. So the state, which organises force when necessary, and appears independent of politics, in fact influences and 'educates' civil society and politics. Political society operates on a terrain that is shaped by the state but functions as the 'mind of the body' of civil society.

"Thomas argues Gramsci's claims that the state is one aspect of civil society, and that civil society also functions as part of the state, are not contradictory at all. The various elements of state and civil society appear independent but are in fact interdependent. This dialectic approach takes us away from pedantic discussions about which institutions fall in to which category. So for example the media appears as separate from the state narrowly defined but in many ways operates as a wing of the state…" [42]

Nineham's specific example, the media, confirms that the issues raised by Anderson remain pertinent. The media in a bourgeois-democratic society – which will include newspapers and websites of the labour movement and the left, as well as dissident and leftish publications of the bourgeoisie – are not at all the same as the media in a fascist or fascistic state. Bourgeois freedom of the press is not just illusion, and not all "the media" in bourgeois-democratic society can be dumped into the same sack. To sink "the media" into a broad "dialectical unity" of the "integral State", "as a wing of the state", is to make that truth much harder to see.

Nineham's keenness to endorse Thomas's argument may be based on an enthusiasm for Thomas's emphasis on the united front as a key idea for Gramsci. Counterfire has made "united fronts" its battle-cry against the SWP majority. However, "united front", for the Counterfire people, is short-hand for a "Munzenberg-type lash-up with Islamic clerical-fascists, or failing that Labour MPs and union bureaucrats, with all political criticism and dialogue stifled, and us pulling the strings in the background". Witness Stop The War, Respect, etc. etc. It has practically nothing in common with Lenin's, Trotsky's, and Gramsci's idea of the united front.

Nineham is certainly garbling Thomas's argument on some points. In *The Gramscian Moment*, the argument goes as follows. The State (in its integral form) should not be understood as limited to the machinery of government and legal institutions (the State in the narrow sense). Rather, the concept of the integral State was intended by Gramsci as a dialectical unity of the moments of civil society and political society.

"Civil society is the terrain upon which social classes compete for social and political leadership or hegemony over other social classes.

Such hegemony is guaranteed, however, 'in the last instance', by capture of the legal monopoly of violence embodied in the institutions of political society" [43].

"Eurocommunists" and "contemporary advocates of a nebulously defined radical democracy" fail to understand this when they "attempt to confine Gramsci's theory of hegemony to a war of position in the trenches of civil society. It is only within the problematic of the integral State as a dialectical unity of both civil society and political society that Gramsci's theory of proletarian hegemony becomes comprehensible, as a theory of the political constitution of an alliance of subaltern classes capable of exercising leadership over other subaltern social groups and repression against its class antagonist, necessarily progressing to the dismantling of the State machinery…" [44].

Hegemony originates in bourgeois society. "Hegemony… emerges as a new 'consensual' political practice distinct from mere coercion (the sole means of previous ruling classes) on this new terrain of civil society; but like civil society, integrally linked to the State, hegemony's full meaning only becomes apparent when it is related to its dialectical distinction of coercion" [45].

Does this mean a picture of civil society as subsumed into the State, so that they merge in an indistinct blur? No. "Gramsci follows Marx by seeing civil society as the true ground of the State, which must now be explained on the basis of the specificity of its transformation of the social forces of civil society into its own forms of political power, rather than [as in Hegel] posited as the necessary and only truth of those social forces. At the same time, however, also following Marx, Gramsci acknowledges that in bourgeois society the State really is primary, in the sense that it is a real abstraction or hypostatisation that subordinates and organises a civil society that, 'enwrapped' by the existing political society, can only figure as its subaltern 'raw material'…" [46].

Is it a slippage when in Gramsci's texts the word "State" comes to denote both the "integral State" ("a dialectical unity of both civil society and political society") and, specifically, "political society"? No.

"Rather than being the result of a confusion, the maintenance of the term State for all dimensions (State in an integral sense, State narrowly conceived as an element of 'political society'), was an attempt to specify that the 'identity-distinction between civil society and political society' occurs 'under the hegemony of the State'. It resulted not in a blurring of the boundaries of the State, but in a clearer delineation of the specific efficacy of the bourgeois State as both a social and a political relation..." [47].

Since civil society and political society form a "dialectical unity", Anderson is also unjust in seeing a tendency within Gramsci to "slip" into a strategy of "civil hegemony" focused in "civil society" as distinct from "political society". "Anderson... assumed, that is, that consent and coercion stand in an antinomian relation to each other, whereas Gramsci's analysis demonstrates in increasingly concrete and precise terms that their relationship can only be rationally comprehended as a dialectical one..." [48].

Gramsci actually envisaged "the dialectical integration of hegemony with domination, of consent with coercion" [49].

Consent and coercion are not "either/or". They are in fact "moments within each other". Civil hegemony is not an alternative to political hegemony. "A bid for 'civil hegemony' has to progress towards 'political hegemony' in order to maintain itself as itself" [50].

Thomas proposes two further arguments about the idea of hegemony in Gramsci. First, that Gramsci based his discussion not so much on the pre-1917 Russian Marxist discussions of "hegemony" (meaning a leading role for the working class in politics, the contrary of "economism") as on Lenin's writings about rebuilding a popular base for the Bolshevik state after the Civil War, in the period of the New Economic Policy [51].

Second, that "the distinctiveness of Gramsci's own concept of hegemony consists precisely in" his concept of "hegemonic apparatus", "this 'micro-concept' of the concrete form in which hegemony is exercised..." "The concept of hegemonic apparatus can therefore be regarded as the 'class-focused' complement to Gramsci's new, 'general notion of the State'. In other words, if the concept of the integral State seeks to delineate the forms and modalities by which a given class stabilises and makes more or less enduring its institutional-political power in political society, the concept of a 'hegemonic apparatus' attempts to chart the ways in which it ascends to power through the intricate network of social relationships of civil society..." [52]

"A class's hegemonic apparatus is the wide-ranging series of institutions (understood in the broadest sense) and practices – from newspapers to educational organisations to political parties – by means of which a class and its allies engage their opponents in a struggle for political power. This concept traverses the boundaries of the so-called public (pertaining to the State) and private (civil society), to include all initiatives by means of which a class concretises its hegemonic project in an integral sense. The hegemonic apparatus is the means by which a class's forces in civil society are translated into power in political society..." [53].

In this context, Thomas tends to dissolve the revolutionary party into "the united front" and "the hegemonic apparatus" as the agency of working-class revolution. Gramsci's distinctive approach, claims Thomas, is "given concrete political expression precisely in his elaboration of the tactic of the United Front into a determining strategic perspective" [54].

This (I think) is what Thomas means when he claims that "the positions proposed by Gramsci cannot be reduced to one or another of those currents that subsequently won (or were spectacularly defeated) in this decisive theoretico-political conjuncture [i.e. Stalinism or the Left Opposition]. Rather, Gramsci proposes positions that are properly seen as a distinctive contribution to these debates, or as attempts to find a dialectical 'third path' beyond the antinomies into which the socialist imagination was then falling..." [55]

"Despite Gramsci's emotionally charged personal reaction to Trotsky, the terms of their analyses are remarkably similar and complementary, in a fitting sense: while Trotsky provides a more detailed analysis of the weakness implicit in the State's omnipotence in the East (as both apparatus and 'political society'), Gramsci's concepts of 'civil society' and 'hegemonic apparatus' provide a more sophisticated theoretical paradigm for grasping the implications for revolutionary strategy of what Trotsky described as the 'heaviest reserves' of the bourgeoisie in the West" [56].

Was Gramsci's central idea the "elaboration of the tactic of the United Front into a determining strategic perspective"? I am not convinced. In any case, I don't think "the United Front" can be a "determining strategic perspective".

As Trotsky wrote: "It was not Lenin who invented the policy of the united front; like the split within the proletariat it is imposed by the dialectics of the class struggle. No successes would be possible without temporary agreements, for the sake of fulfilling immediate tasks, among various sections, organisations, and groups of the proletariat. Strikes, trade unions, journals, parliamentary elections, street demonstrations, demand that the split be bridged in practice from time to time as the need arises; that is, they demand an ad hoc united front, even if it does not always take on the form of one. In the first stages of a movement, unity arises episodically and spontaneously from below, but when the masses are accustomed to fighting through their organizations, unity must also be established at the top. Under the conditions existing in advanced capitalist countries, the slogan of 'only from below' is a gross anachronism, fostered by memories of the first stages of the revolutionary movement, especially in Czarist Russia.

"At a certain level, the struggle for unity of action is converted from an elementary fact into a tactical task. The simple formula of the united front solves nothing. It is not only Communists who appeal for unity, but also reformists, and even fascists. The tactical application of the united front is subordinated, in every given period, to a definite strategic conception…" [57]

Trotsky made similar points in his argument, after October 1923, that the Brandler-Thalheimer leadership of the Communist Party of Germany had become dazzled or pixillated into thinking "united front" a sufficient strategy. In other words: a revolutionary party must engage in a complex system of united fronts – constantly adjusted and revised class-based alliances, with internal dialogue and criticism, to deal with different issues. It needs a whole system of organisations, initiatives, campaigns, themes of agitation, all focused around the two tasks of self-education of the organised working class and establishing the organised working class as the leader of broader plebeian layers. But all the different united fronts cannot be subsumed into a single strategic imperative of "the" united front.

And what of the linking of the "united front" with the political orientation of Lenin in his last writings about the government of the USSR? Those later writings in Lenin were focused on anxious attempts to civilise the state that had emerged from the civil war and now had to make its way amidst economic ruin, the sullen hostility of very large sections of the peasantry, and the tiredness and scattering of the industrial working class. They were concerned – as all Bolsheviks were in the early 1920s – to maintain the link ("smychka") between working class and peasantry, but proposed no united front of any sort remotely comparable to that advocated in Western Europe, because Lenin at that point could not see his way clear to any slackening of the Bolsheviks' political monopoly, or even to a comprehensive re-enlivening of the Bolshevik party. The Left Opposition in 1923 would see more clearly than Lenin, but even they can be seen with hindsight to have been – understandably, and perhaps inevitably – slow in understanding the full significance of the congealing of a bureaucratic caste, and perplexed and cautious in their proposals against it. Neither they, nor Lenin in his last months, conceived of themselves as developing model proposals for an expansive and sensitive system of working-class democracy; they were scrabbling for makeshift, patch-up policies in a situation they saw as desperate and doomed to remain desperate until workers' revolutions in more advanced countries came to their aid.

Lenin: "The most harmful thing would be to rely on the assumption that we know at least something, or that we have any considerable number of elements necessary for the building of a really new state apparatus, one really worthy to be called socialist, Soviet, etc. No, we are ridiculously deficient of such an apparatus, and even of the elements of it, and we must remember that we should not stint time on building it, and that it will take many, many years". [58].

The NEP and the united front were seen by many – especially the "left communists" who opposed both – as kindred moves away from the hectic rushed assaults of "war communism" in the USSR and the immediate uprisings in the West of 1919; but they were not the same thing.

I fear that Thomas has stretched the term "united front" into something too broad. And in his discussion of the "integral State", I fear that the word "dialectical" has been given too much work to do, more than it will bear and more than Gramsci himself assigns to that adjective. Civil society and political society, so Peter Thomas asserts, are not different areas of society, but only different moments of the "dialectical unity of both" in the integral State. They can be distinguished from each other, but only "methodologically". Consent and coercion, hegemony and domination, are "dialectically integrated".

This generality glosses over one of Anderson's main points: that there is a specific form of interrelation of civil society and State in bourgeois democracy. It is one which includes boundaries between the two – a relative separation of politics and economics, and of public and private. The fallacy of all sorts of syndicalism – the "cultural syndicalism", in Thomas's apt phrase, and ordinary trade-union syndicalism – is generally not that they are so foolish as to forget about the problem of "political hegemony" altogether, but, in effect, that they take the proposition "a bid for 'civil hegemony' has to progress towards 'political hegemony' in order to maintain itself as itself" (Thomas, p.194) as a description of a process guaranteed by the "dialectical unity" of these things to come about in due course, rather than as an imperative for specifically political initiative.

The relative separation of politics and economics, and of public and private, in bourgeois democracy, allows the working class to win what Trotsky described as "bases of proletarian democracy" within bourgeois society. If all institutions are lumped together into one "dialectical unity" of the "integral State", then this built-in tension, the development of which is vital to working-class politics, is lost from sight, or at least shielded from sight.

"In a developed capitalist society, during a democratic regime, the bourgeoisie leans for support primarily upon the working classes, which are held in check by the reformists. In its most finished form, this system finds its expression in Britain during the administration of the Labour government as well as during that of the Conservatives. In a fascist regime, at least during its first phase, capital leans on the petty bourgeoisie, which destroys the organisations of the proletariat. Italy, for instance!

"Is there a difference in the 'class content' of these two regimes? If the question is posed only as regards the ruling class, then there is no difference. If one takes into account the position and the interrelations of all classes, from the angle of the proletariat, then the difference appears to be quite enormous.

"In the course of many decades, the workers have built up within the bourgeois democracy, by utilising it, by fighting against it, their own strongholds and bases of proletarian democracy: the trade unions, the political parties, the educational and sport clubs, the cooperatives, etc. The proletariat cannot attain power within the formal limits of bourgeois democracy, but can do so only by taking the road of revolution: this has been proved both by theory and experience. And these bulwarks of workers' democracy within the bourgeois state are absolutely essential for taking the revolutionary road. The work of the Second International consisted in creating just such bulwarks during the epoch when it was still fulfilling its progressive historic labour.

"Fascism has for its basic and only task the razing to their foundations of all institutions of proletarian democracy...." [59].

Trotsky was writing about Germany on the eve of Hitler's seizure of power. In a situation of relatively stable bourgeois democracy, Trotsky's concepts here point to the need for a struggle for the *transformation of the mass labour movement* into an agency of revolutionary activity.

This can be conceptualised, and maybe fruitfully, as a struggle for the creation of a working-class "hegemonic apparatus". But to write about "the concept of a 'hegemonic apparatus' [as] chart[ing] the ways in which [a given class] ascends to power through the intricate network of social relationships of civil society…" [60] is to mystify the tasks. The working class is not a "given class", which then "ascends through" an intricate network. A great part of the task is, so to speak, to "give" the working class to itself – to bring together, within and by utilising certain defined parts of the "intricate network" of civil society, dispersed groups of workers as a class-conscious collective with its own independent will and organisation.

The other shore of Gramsci's bridge: Gramsci and "post-Marxism"

Martin Thomas

ANTONIO GRAMSCI WAS a revolutionary Marxist of the early-1920s Lenin-Trotsky stripe. Yet his prison writings of 1929-35 have been used as a source for quite different politics.

First, the Italian Communist Party (PCI), which had cold-shouldered Gramsci in prison as his criticism of Stalinist policies emerged, took him up from the early 1950s and especially in the 1960s. The PCI took Gramsci's discussions of "hegemony" and "war of position" as justifying class-collaboration and an idea of transforming society by gradually winning more and more influence (especially, in practice, in local government).

Gramsci's writings reached the English-speaking world through a short book of extracts published by the British Communist Party in 1957, after Khrushchev's startling anti-Stalin speech of 1956, and via the "New Left" in the early 1960s. For example, in *Towards Socialism*, a collection of essays published by New Left Review in 1965, Perry Anderson referred to Gramsci in order to argue a strategy supposedly based on "hegemony" and supposedly "going beyond" Leninism and social democracy. The main practical recommendation in Anderson's article was to urge the Labour Party to boost or to organise Labour-aligned associations among lawyers, doctors, scientists, teachers, and "every intellectual group".

In the late 1970s and the 1980s, Gramsci was often cited by Communist Parties pursuing a new "Eurocommunist" line to try to rid themselves of the taint of Stalinism. Since the collapse of the Communist Parties, Gramsci has been a source for a "post-Marxism", advocating "radical democracy" rather than even notionally working-class politics.

Probably as a result, Gramsci has remained a widely-cited and widely-taught author in universities, while Lenin, Trotsky, Luxemburg and the like have not. There is now a vast volume of "post-Gramscian" studies.

There is nothing new about the texts of a revolutionary writer being used, once he or she is safely dead, to gloss unrevolutionary politics. The operation is easier with Gramsci since his *Prison Notebooks* were fragmentary, never finalised for publication, and often cryptic in style.

Many Marxist writers have shown that Gramsci did not change his fundamental revolutionary Marxist views in prison (1926-37) and while writing his *Prison Notebooks* (1929-35). However, the post-Marxists do not deny that they have "gone beyond" Gramsci. They do not particularly claim to be loyal to Gramsci. Their argument is, so to speak, that the "other shore" of the theoretical "bridge" to new thinking provided by Gramsci's writings is their "radical democratic" politics, even though Gramsci himself would not have seen or wanted that.

Richard Bellamy, an important writer in the same political spectrum as the "post-Marxists" — though he prefers the banner, "realist liberalism" — edited a useful volume of Gramsci's pre-prison writings, and agrees that most of the central concepts of the *Prison Notebooks* were also in the pre-prison writings. But he concludes that what Gramsci adapted from the liberal (and one-time Marxisant) philosopher Benedetto Croce is sounder than Gramsci's criticisms of Croce — in other words, that Gramsci is valuable for what of Croce has filtered through him, rather than for what differentiated him from Croce.

"The recent post-Marxist reading of Gramsci can be regarded as an implicit return to [the] Crocean radical alternative", writes Bellamy [61]; but, for him, that is a merit, not a fault, of "post-Marxism". To answer Bellamy by demonstrating that Gramsci was not a "post-Marxist" is not to answer him.

The central concept in all the discussions has been what Gramsci called "hegemony". Before 1917, Russian Marxists saw themselves as fighting for "hegemony", meaning the organisation of the working class so that it could take a leading role in (have hegemony in) the democratic revolt of multiple sectors of the Russian empire's people against Tsarist autocracy, and specifically of the peasant revolt. They counterposed that approach to "economism", the perspective of those socialists who wanted to focus on agitation and organisation around immediate working-class economic struggles, were willing to leave the other struggles to the bourgeois liberals, and reckoned that working-class politics could develop spontaneously out of the working-class economic struggles.

Some writers have argued that Gramsci first took the idea of "hegemony" from Italian writers such as Croce, before becoming aware of the Russian Marxists' discussions; but for sure Gramsci considered Lenin's ideas on hegemony important. In the *Prison Notebooks* he strove to develop those ideas, and to construct what he saw as the strategic vision underlying and exemplified in the tactic of the united front argued for by Lenin and Trotsky, against much opposition, in the Communist Parties in 1921-2.

The bourgeoisie had ruled — so Gramsci argued — and the working class must prepare itself to rule, not just by pursuing sectional interests, but by generating political parties which construct a "hegemonic apparatus": a complex of organisations, united-fronts, interventions, themes of agitation, etc. which enable the fundamental class to see itself as a leader, or potential leader, of society, and which offer other groups an effective alliance.

The political party must polemicise against its opponents not by cheap shots — just picking on their weakest advocates, or just "exposing" petty corruption and mercenary motives — but by tackling their best and strongest advocates, thus achieving an expansive influence among thinking people.

Rather than dawdling with the assurance that underlying economic laws would duly rally people to it in time, the political party must constantly be creative in political initiative. The economic impulse, powerful though it be, always requires a suitable political initiative to express it. The party's "perspective" cannot be a mechanical calculation from broad economic and historical trends, but must count the party's own intervention as a creative factor. The "perspective" is not mechanical prediction, but an always-conditional guide to action. The revolutionary working-class party should not assume it faces an immobile enemy. There are periods of "passive revolution" in which the ruling class transforms society, in its own way and in its own interests, and meanwhile channels and stifles subaltern sections of the population in new ways. And the party itself must be a continuous process of self-creation, working to make all its members "intellectuals", rather than utilising the Catholic Church's method of uniting educated strata with the less-lettered, i.e. of imposing rigid dogmatic limits on the educated.

In Gramsci's writings these ideas are counterposed to the traditional "workerist" and "trade-unionist" and politically-passive "maximalism" of the Italian Socialist Party; to the more intransigent and apocalyptic version of similar ideas proposed by the Italian Communist Party's first leader, Amadeo Bordiga; and to the cursory polemics and "statistical"-materialist sociology of a Marxist handbook by Bukharin. When Gramsci argued, however, that "an appropriate political initiative is always necessary to liberate the economic thrust from the dead weight of traditional policies", he also believed that there was an underlying, shaping, structuring "economic thrust", and that the initiative must come from a class-based force. The question is: was he wrong on that?

The Italian Communist Party adapted Gramsci's ideas by fading out the working-class basis of hegemony and Gramsci's assumption that hegemony could be won only by a bold, militant working-class movement. They transformed "hegemony" into a code-word for repeated recyclings of the "Popular Front" approach of the Communist Parties in the late 1930s, when they formally renounced the political independence of the working class in favour of alliances with miscellaneous bourgeois forces supposed to "stop fascism" as a "first stage" after which direct working-class causes might be taken up in a "second stage".

In 1926 Gramsci, puzzled by the factional dispute in Russia, had complained about the Stalinists' bureaucratic abuses against the Left Opposition, but was inclined to credit the argument of Stalin and Bukharin that their policy represented a restraint on direct working-class and socialist drive necessary in order to keep an alliance with the peasantry — in other words, that the Left Opposition showed a "residue of reformist or syndicalist corporativism". Such arguments, mistaken I believe, could be seized on by the PCI to rationalise restraining working-class combativity on the grounds that such combativity would spoil the alliance with middle-class groups necessary to win a majority. Paradoxically, the PCI was able to transform Gramsci's ideas about the revolutionary party's responsibility to be creative, to take initiative, and to educate, into a rationalisation for a notoriously stodgy, passive, routinist policy, pursued by a very bureaucratic party in a very manipulative way.

In the ideology of the Italian Communist Party, however, the whole approach was still, at least notionally and in some supposed last analysis, tied to a specifically working-class project. The working class was admitted to have distinct immediate and historic interests, and any shelving of those for the sake of alliances was (at least notionally) presumed to be temporary.

In the mid-1970s and the early 1980s, the Italian CP ideology, reformulated to include a marked distancing from the USSR, acquired wide international influence under the name "Eurocommunism". This was the way that the Communist Parties tried to adapt both to a new generation of radicalised youth and to the distrust by those youth and by older activists of the model of the USSR.

Eurocommunism was said to be a new alternative both to Leninism (read: Stalinism) and to social democracy. The links of a strategy of "hegemony" with the working class were faded out further, though still not completely (in formal terms anyway). The Communist Parties attempted, rather clumsily, to court the "new social movements" (feminist, lesbian-gay, anti-nuclear, etc.); and the political goal was posed as intervening "within as well as against the state", transforming it gradually rather than confronting it, capturing it, or using it as an already-given instrument.

The British version of Eurocommunism argued that Margaret Thatcher's Tories had developed a successful "hegemonic project", ideologically capturing great sections of the working class, with the conclusion (even before the miners' defeat in 1985) that direct working-class struggle had no real prospects.

Eurocommunism's flowering was brief. By the early 1990s the Eurocommunist parties had mostly dissolved themselves, or radically shrunk, and most of the Eurocommunist ideologues had moved on. The "post-Marxist" follow-up to Eurocommunism was pioneered in an article in the British Communist Party journal *Marxism Today*, in January 1981, by Ernesto Laclau and Chantal Mouffe.

Laclau and Mouffe were academics — of Argentinian and Belgian origin, respectively, but settled in Britain — not members of the Communist Party, but in its orbit, and previously admirers of the French Communist Party philosopher Louis Althusser. From Althusser they valued above all his emphasis on the "relative autonomy" of politics and ideology. They found in Gramsci a similar emphasis — and, they thought, the means to move from "relative autonomy" to straight autonomy.

Laclau and Mouffe first presented their ideas as radically left-wing. In their January 1981 article they criticised the Italian CP as being too stodgy to relate to the "new social movements", and condemned the excessive "concessions to the class enemy" of pre-1914 Marxist parties. Thirty years later, they still consider themselves left-wing. Mouffe denounces the "third way", "beyond left and right" ideas of writers like the New Labour ideologue Anthony Giddens, and insists: "Right and left are still fundamental categories of politics". She criticises New Labour as having oriented to the middle class and abandoned workers. Despite describing her politics now as "radical democratic" rather than socialist, she denounces neo-liberalism and advocates "different modes of regulation of market forces" (albeit not their subjugation), "basic income", a shorter working week, etc.

Laclau and Mouffe are also clear than they reject Marxism. In the 1981 article their argument was posed as a call for a "Copernican revolution" within Marxism, but by 1985 they described their views as post-Marxist. They are also avowedly "post-Gramscian". They retained the "broad democratic alliance" orientation which went back to the Italian CP of decades before, but amputated all the notional connections to class struggle, economic determination, and revolution.

Their basic step was to extrapolate "relative autonomy" to full autonomy — and more. Even in Gramsci, they now argued, lurked remnants of "economism" and of an old-Marxist model of society in which one part ("superstructure" — ideology, politics) expresses or reflects another (the economic "base").

They argued that the "base-superstructure" concept should be completely rejected. The argument proceeded by leaps. Social life is the action of individuals and groups, none of which are mechanically determined by economic conditions. Yes; but aren't the overall directions of social life, and the alternatives which emerge in it, shaped and often "statistically" determined by the economic relations which structure production and distribution, people's working lives, and much of their conditions outside work too? No, said Laclau and Mouffe. *In fact, they came close to inverting the "base-superstructure" idea, rather than simply rejecting it.*

"There does not exist an essence of the social order beyond a political relation of forces". "Political struggle [is] constitutive of the social order". "All social phenomena and objects can only acquire meaning within a discourse". "Identities — lacking any essence — are formed through political struggle". "Politico-hegemonic articulations retroactively create the interests they claim to represent". We have to recognise "the primacy of politics" even "within the economy itself". In other words, the shaping of social life is nothing but the workings of "hegemonic" techniques, free-floating from any economic or class underpinning. Those "hegemonic" techniques create the economic or interest-group underpinning, rather than being shaped by it.

They redefined hegemony as "a process of the production of popular-democratic subjects", a "political articulation of different identities into a common project", or a process whereby "a particular social force assumes the representation of a totality that is radically incommensurable with it", or more simply just as "processes which can bring people together".

Gramsci's concept of hegemony — and Lenin's — involved some element of compromise, of bringing together different plebeian groups in an alliance shaped by definite core interests but also allowing room for divergences and disputes. Laclau and Mouffe moved on from that to the idea of "agonistic pluralism" as the central goal of political action. The goal is to construct a "radical democracy" in which different groups relate as "adversaries" — with mutual accommodation, dialogue, etc. — rather than as "enemies".

The core task for left-wingers is to construct a "chain of equivalence" which can bring together diverse causes into an alliance where each considers itself equally valued.

The chain is not quite all-embracing: "A chain of equivalence needs... a critical frontier. For a hegemony to have a radical focus, it needs to establish an enemy, be it capitalism, ecological destruction, or violation of human rights". But it must be broad and loose. We must reject the "very idea of a privileged subject" — that the working class, or any other pre-defined group, is determined as the core agency of change.

With that, we must reject the idea of comprehensive revolution. Laclau's and Mouffe's "organising principles are the democratic ideas of equality and liberty for all", and their goal is not revolution but "a radicalisation of ideas and values which [are] already present, although unfulfilled, in liberal capitalism" [62].

As well as being "post-Marxist", they want to be "post-Jacobin" (though they do not use that term). In Jacobinism, the ideology of the radical wing of the French Revolution — in Marxism, too, and in some varieties of liberalism which they reject — they see an excessive rationalism, an impossible drive to meld the whole of society into a single collective will. Insisting on the necessary partial and piecemeal nature of political action, they argue that "post-Marxism" must eschew the idea of revolution found in Marxism, as well as the ideas of economic base, class, and class interest.

The 1985 book in which Laclau and Mouffe codified their ideas — *Hegemony and Socialist Strategy* — made clear in its first pages that this direction in their thought was governed by revulsion against Stalinism. They cited the Russian invasion of Afghanistan (1979), the suppression of the Polish workers in 1981, the horrors following Stalinist victory in Vietnam and Cambodia (after 1975) as facts requiring a rethink of Marxism. Like many others, they had taken the Stalinist states as more or less good coin, as more or less exemplars of revolutionary working-class socialist rule, and thus wanted to find new left-wing politics that, rejecting Stalinism, would also reject working-class socialist revolution.

Laclau and Mouffe comment that they see much of their approach as having been prefigured by a section of the pre-1914 Marxist movement, the so-called "Austro-Marxists" (ideologues of the Austrian Marxist movement of that time). They must have in mind the idea of a democratic order put together from "cultural-national autonomy", with an elaborate complex of mutually adjusting institutions for the various national groups in the mosaic of the pre-World-War-One Austro-Hungarian empire.

Over the last 25 years ideas like Laclau's and Mouffe's have spawned a vast literature. In the 2001 introduction to the second edition of *Hegemony and Socialist Strategy*, Laclau and Mouffe seek to refer to, and draw support for their ideas from, a range of writings including those of Wittgenstein, Heidegger, Feyerabend, and Lacan. A lot of Mouffe's recent writing has been in the form of critique of the right-wing political philosopher Carl Schmitt. However, we can do more than gasp in awe at the length of the bibliographies. We can make some political assessment of the current represented by "post-Marxism".

Like many other schools of thought, their ideas were built on trends which appeared factually solid and well-established at the time they first wrote, but which were soon to disappear. In 1981, one of Laclau's and Mouffe's key arguments was that the economic base of capitalism was not determining politics, but, on the contrary, different politics in different places were visibly shaping society in decisively different ways. "The reorganisation of capitalism... increasingly depends on forms of political articulation which affect the supposed 'laws of motion'...."

The first talk of "hegemony" as the guiding principle in politics, they argued, had come after World War One when a "new mass character of political struggle", "Lloyd-Georgism" — presumably they mean a general shift towards more populist politics, away from the assured continual domination of traditional elites — had supposedly "obliged socialist politics to adopt a popular and democratic character... totally incompatible with the [alleged] strict 'class-ism' of Kautsky or Plekhanov". Eurocommunism they saw as a forced recognition of "the far-reaching transformations" of capitalist societies "consequent upon Keynesian economic policies", for example the broadening of the state to include numerous welfare institutions.

By 1981 Keynesian economic policies were already being discarded by the leading governments. At least, they were being discarded in the form common in the 1960s and 70s. Despite the brief vogues of monetarism and "supply-side economics", the ruling classes did not in fact forget Keynes's insights, as they would show in their response to crisis in 2008. But with the increasing integration of almost all countries into an increasingly fast-moving and fluid capitalist world market, even the "relative" autonomy of politics has been much reduced. Bourgeois welfare-populism of a 1960s-Keynesian or Lloyd-George sort has been marginalised. Governments everywhere, of all parties, pursue much the same neoliberal policies. They are explicit about being subject to the "economic base". "You can't buck the markets". Tony Blair told us that adjusting the Labour Party to the new era meant making it the party, not of some newly-constructed "popular-democratic subject", but "of business". In Britain, and in many other countries, this process of making politics much more a servant of "the economic base", so to speak, has been openly institutionalised by transferring a large part of state economic decision-making to a central bank mandated to be independent from parliament or government.

The "autonomy", or the economy-shaping role, of the political is markedly less than before 1980 — and less than when Gramsci, or Trotsky, or Lenin, were writing, or when Marx was writing and exclaimed: "The 'present-day' state is... a fiction... [It] changes with a country's frontier. It is different in the Prusso-German Empire from what it is in Switzerland, and different in England from what it is in the United States" [63]. Neither Marx, nor the great revolutionary Marxists, ever thought that the state simply "expressed" the "economic base", or did not reciprocally influence it. Perhaps the only ostensible Marxists who thought that were the Stalinists who said that the USSR's governing machine must be "socialist" because it was "based" on a nationalised economy.

There is still scope today for individual governments to act differently — in fact, much more scope than they admit. There are still governments which (while going a long way with the general neo-liberal flow) flout the dominant world political trend, though in a malign rather than benign way: Iran, for one. But, especially in the core areas of world capitalism, the "autonomy of politics" is visibly much reduced.

Mouffe is aware of this. She calls our times "post-political", is alarmed by this, and comments ruefully that much of the task today has to be not to press for more radical democracy, but to defend such democratic institutions that exist.

The organised working class and the labour movement are at a lower ebb than in 1981. We have suffered from successive defeats followed by a hectic surge of capitalist economic restructuring, and the ground on which to rebuild socialist politics is still poisoned by Stalinism. But the organised working class and the labour movement still exist, and the "parties of business" still acknowledge that they are fighting a battle chiefly against that enemy.

What of the "new social movements" which Laclau and Mouffe thought must banish from our minds all ideas of a single class movement as central? In fact they have ebbed more than the organised working class. Some of them have a vigorous sort of after-life in NGOs. But Mouffe does not pretend that NGO politics, or the localised and one-off activism more common today, is a real vehicle for hegemony: she criticises as illusory the perspectives of those who "want a pure movement of civil society" and "do not want to have anything to do with existing institutions such as parties and trade unions".

"Post-Marxism" has had a very wide diffusion. But as a perspective for the left to recover from the defeats of the late 1970s and 1980s, it cannot claim to have had much grip.

Since the 1980s, a barebones form of bourgeois parliamentary democracy has spread much more widely, to ex-Stalinist Eastern Europe and to most of Latin America for example. That bourgeois parliamentary democracy has simultaneously been more and more hollowed out in its established heartlands — by restrictions on the democratic rights of labour, by the loss of civil liberties (especially in the "war on terror"), and by the increasing transformation of politics into a game played by professional political careerists, think-tanks, and media people, propelled by financing from the wealthy and big business, above the heads of the electorate. The "post-Marxists" are influential people. What have they done, or even proposed, to reverse that trend?

Perhaps more than any time in history, the last 25 years prove that a battle for democratic forms is ineffectual if not tied together with a socialist battle to reorganise the working-class as an assertive, militant combatant for its own interests, as the champion of democracy, and as the leader of all the oppressed and plebeians.

Gramsci and Trotsky

Martin Thomas

IN JUNE 1930 Alfonso Leonetti, Paolo Ravazzoli, and Pietro Tresso — three of the eight members of the Executive of the Italian Communist Party — were expelled. Stalin was imposing in Italy his "Third Period" line which had led the German Communist Party to denounce the Social Democrats as "social fascists" and dismiss the threat of Hitler taking power (it said "fascism" was already in power, and another form of "fascism" could thus be no new threat; and anyway, "after Hitler, our turn next").

Italian fascism had been in power since 1922, and since about 1926 had snuffed out all legal labour-movement activity in Italy. Leonetti, Ravazzoli, and Tresso wanted to campaign for bourgeois-democratic demands against the fascist regime, and to challenge social democracy with united-front proposals rather than complacently declaring that social democracy was already dead and the future was single combat between the Communist Party and fascism. The three formed the "New Italian Opposition", the first Italian Trotskyist group.

Since 1927 the Italian CP had been led by Palmiro Togliatti, an ingenious and supple-spined politician who remained in post and in line with Moscow until his death in 1964. Before Togliatti the main leader had been Antonio Gramsci. From 8 November 1926 Gramsci had been isolated in fascist jails; but his brother Gennaro could visit him. According to Antonio Gramsci's orthodox Communist Party biographer, Giuseppe Fiori: "Antonio... supported the attitude of Leonetti, Tresso, and Ravazzoli... and rejected the International's new policy".

Gennaro went back to Togliatti, in exile, "and told him Nino [Antonio] was in complete agreement with him... Had I told a different story, not even Nino would have been saved from expulsion" [64]. Antonio

Gramsci was cold-shouldered by the CP until he died in 1937, and taken up again as a hero only later, in the 1950s, when Togliatti could safely use him as a symbol of a "national" orientation without clashing with Moscow.

In 1932, trying to rouse the German workers' movement to united action against Hitler, and to learn the lessons of the crushing of the Italian workers by fascism, Trotsky cited Gramsci as a model of sober revolutionary-socialist politics. "Italian comrades inform me that with the sole exception of Gramsci, the Communist Party wouldn't even allow of the possibility of the fascists seizing power... Once the proletarian revolution had suffered defeat... how could there be any further kind of counterrevolutionary upheaval? The bourgeoisie cannot rise up against itself! Such was the gist of the political orientation of the Italian Communist Party" [10].

Gramsci and Trotsky had met when Gramsci went to Russia between May 1922 and December 1923, for the Fourth Congress of the Communist International and other meetings. In 1922 Gramsci was still deferring to Amadeo Bordiga, the main leader of the Italian Communist Party, and Bordiga's opposition to political united-front tactics and to broadening out the CP. But Gramsci's writings in 1919 and 1920 had shown a more dialectical turn of mind. As Frank Rosengarten records [65], to Trotsky and others, Gramsci "seemed... to be the man best suited to liberate the Italian party from the fruitless rigidities of... Bordiga". Trotsky later told another Italian Communist: "We had to press hard to convince him [Gramsci] to take a combative position against Bordiga and I don't know whether we succeeded".

"Hard", from a Trotsky fresh from the Russian civil war and convinced that failure to shift to united-front policies could wreck the young Communist Parties and bring isolation and collapse to the Russian workers' republic, meant *hard*. Gramsci was probably bruised, but over the next years he started arguing for united-front policies and against Bordiga. In his *Prison Notebooks* he continued to explore the issue. His agreement with Ravazzoli, Leonetti, and Tresso in 1930 reflected a conviction by then long and solidly held.

Trotsky at the Fourth Congress also gave Gramsci another theme which he would explore in the *Prison Notebooks*: the differences for revolutionary-socialist politics between a Western Europe with densely-organised civil societies, where socialists would have to tackle "heavy reserves" of the bourgeoisie before revolution, and a more loosely-knit

Russia. Some writers on Gramsci have claimed that he deduced from that difference a policy for richer capitalist societies of gradual advance through cultural diffusion, in place of the activist party politics of the Bolsheviks in Russia. That deduction would have been as out of character for Gramsci as for Trotsky.

Trotsky: "In Europe we have a process differing profoundly from that in our country, because there the bourgeoisie is far better organised and more experienced, because there the petty-bourgeoisie has graduated from the school of the big bourgeoisie and is, in consequence, also far more powerful and experienced; and, in addition, the Russian Revolution has taught them a good deal...

"[In Russia] the big bourgeoisie and the nobility had gained some political experience, thanks to the municipal dumas, the zemstvos, the state Duma, etc. The petty bourgeoisie had little political experience, and the bulk of the population, the peasantry, still less. Thus the main reserves of the counter-revolution — the well-to-do peasants (kulaks) and, to a degree, also the middle peasants — came precisely from this extremely amorphous milieu. And it was only after the bourgeoisie began to grasp fully what it had lost by losing political power, and only after it had set in motion its counter-revolutionary combat nucleus, that it succeeded in gaining access to the peasant and petty-bourgeois elements and layers...

"In countries that are older in the capitalist sense, and with a higher culture, the situation will, without doubt, differ profoundly. In these countries the popular masses will enter the revolution far more fully formed in political respects... The bourgeoisie in the West is preparing its counter-blow in advance. The bourgeoisie more or less knows what elements it will have to depend upon and it builds its counter-revolutionary cadres in advance...

"It will hardly be possible to catch the European bourgeoisie by surprise as we caught the Russian bourgeoisie. The European bourgeoisie is more intelligent, and more farsighted... The revolutionary proletariat will thus encounter on its road to power not only the combat vanguards of the counter-revolution but also its heaviest reserves...

"But by way of compensation, after the proletarian overturn... the European proletariat will in all likelihood have far more elbow room for its creative work in economy and culture than we had in Russia... This general proposition must be dissected and concretised with regard to each country depending upon its social structure..." [66]

Gramsci wrote an essay on Italian futurism included in Trotsky's book *Literature and Revolution*. Later, "the positions that Gramsci was to take on the relations between art and politics in the *Prison Notebooks* are... remarkably similar to those taken by Trotsky in the years 1923 and 1924, when he... led the campaign... to 'reject party tutelage over science and art'." (Rosengarten [65])

From Moscow, Gramsci went to Vienna, where he worked with Victor Serge, an activist in the Left Opposition to Stalin which emerged, around Trotsky, in 1923-4. Serge recalled in his memoirs that Gramsci was wary of the flood of careerist recruits brought into the Russian CP by Stalin and his allies after Lenin's death in the same way that the Left Opposition was. "Trained intuitively in the dialectic, quick to uncover falsehood and transfix it with the sting of irony, [Gramsci] viewed the world with exceptional clarity. Once, we consulted together about the quarter-million workers who had been admitted at one stroke into the Russian Communist Party on the day after Lenin's death [in 1924]. How much were these proletarians worth, if they had had to wait for the death of Vladimir Ilyich before coming to the Party... When the crisis in Russia [between the Left Opposition and Stalin] began to worsen, Gramsci did not want to be broken in the process, so he had himself sent back to Italy by his Party" [67]. (Taking his seat in the Italian parliament, won in the April 1924 election, must have been the main motive. Gramsci may well also have been glad to get further afield from the Comintern centre).

Gramsci and Trotsky were both revolutionary Marxists. Yet Gramsci was not a Trotskyist, and Trotsky was not a Gramscian. What were their differences, and what can we learn from them?

In February 1924 Gramsci had declared that the Left Opposition stood for "a greater measure of involvement on the part of the workers in the life of the party and a lessening of the powers of the bureaucracy, in order to assure to the revolution its socialist and working-class character" [68]. In a letter sent to Stalin's Central Committee just before he was jailed in 1926, Gramsci still protested at Stalin's bureaucratism, and for that reason the pliant Togliatti, then living in Moscow, suppressed the letter. But Gramsci now also went along with the demagogic argument from Stalin and Bukharin that the Joint Opposition of 1926-7 (drawing in Zinoviev and Kamenev as well as the 1923 Oppositionists) represented an economistic or workerist failure to understand the concessions necessary to the peasantry.

"In the ideology and practice of the opposition bloc is being fully reborn the entire tradition of social democracy and syndicalism which has thus far prevented the Western proletariat from organising itself into a ruling class" [69].

Gramsci was wrong on that: Stalin's turn within two years to murderous terror against both the peasantry and the working class is ample proof.

In the *Prison Notebooks* Gramsci continued to conflate Trotsky's ideas with very different ones. "[Trotsky] can be considered the political theorist of frontal attack in a period in which it only leads to defeats" [70] .

Was Gramsci conflating Trotsky with the people in the early Communist Parties who said that revolutionary principle demanded a permanent "offensive"? But Trotsky had been the main polemicist against them.

Was he conflating Trotsky with Trotsky's ally in the 1926-7 United Opposition, Zinoviev, who in 1924-5 (in alliance, then, with Stalin) had pushed a blustering ultra-left line onto the Communist International? Zinoviev had declared in January 1924: "What is Italian Social Democracy? It is a wing of the Fascists. Turati is a Fascist Social Democrat. Could we have said this five years ago? ... Ten years ago we had opportunists, but could we say that they were Fascist Social Democrats? No. It would have been absurd to say it then. Now, however, they are Fascists... The international Social Democracy has now become a wing of Fascism." [71] But Trotsky had been the main polemicist against that line, too, and the formation of the United Opposition represented a sharp shift by Zinoviev.

Was he conflating Trotsky's ideas with those of Bordiga, who in 1926 was the most vocal supporter from outside Russia of the United Opposition, bravely confronting Stalin face-to-face at the Executive of the Comintern in that year? Although Trotsky respected Bordiga, he differed from him on issues like the united front.

Even more oddly, Gramsci in the *Prison Notebooks* referred back to Trotsky's speeches at the Fourth Congress of 1922, and then dismissed Trotsky with a sneer. "However, the question was outlined only in a brilliant, literary form, without directives of a practical character" [72]. Trotsky had explained very well the "directives of a practical character", and the folly of permanent "frontal attack" — including to the initially-resistant Gramsci himself.

The early German Communist Party, explained Trotsky, "still felt as if it were a shell shot out of a cannon. It appeared on the scene and it seemed to it that it needed only shout its battle-cry, dash forward and the working class would rush to follow. It turned out otherwise...

"The working class had been deceived more than once in the past, it has every reason to demand that the party win its confidence... the need [was] for the Communists to conquer, in experience, in practice, in struggle, the confidence of the working class... A new epoch [of communist activity was necessary] which at first glance contains much that is, so to speak, prosaic, namely — agitation, propaganda, organization, conquest of the confidence of the workers in the day-to-day struggles".

The Communist Parties had to learn again, and adapt, much that was of enduring value from the tactics of the pre-1914 Marxist movement. "Some comrades told us: And where is the guarantee that this organisational-agitational-educational work will not degenerate into the very same reformism, along the road travelled by the Second International? No guarantees are handed us from the outside. The guarantees arise from our work, our criticism, our self-criticism and our control" [73].

United-front tactics were central to the "prosaic" work. "We must conquer the confidence of the overwhelming majority of the toilers. This can and must be achieved in the course of struggle for the transitional demands under the general slogan of the proletarian united front" [74].

In his writings on Germany in the 1930s, Trotsky would further explain that in advanced capitalist countries, with dense civil societies, the united front "from above" — agitation and organisation around demands directed at established reformist leaderships — was almost always an essential component. "Under the conditions existing in advanced capitalist countries, the slogan of 'only from below' is a gross anachronism, fostered by memories of the first stages of the revolutionary movement, especially in Czarist Russia" [57].

Why did Gramsci "forget" all that? Trotsky was on the defensive in 1925, waiting quietly for a better occasion to rouse revolutionary opinion against Stalinism. Maybe that disoriented Gramsci. We cannot know. In the *Prison Notebooks* — written, of course, in conditions when Gramsci had access to only a few of Trotsky's writings, and those with difficulty — Gramsci left his odd depiction of Trotsky as an ideologue of reckless "frontal attack" only asserted, not argued. Frank Rosengarten conjectures that in 1924-6 two "considerations weighed heavily on Gramsci and impelled him towards the condemnation of Trotskyism as factious and insubordinate". One was "the need to create a compactly organised, tightly disciplined, and ideologically unified Communist Party in Italy";

the other, "his belief that if the dispute in the Soviet Union were to go on without a resolution of some sort, it would spell the doom of the entire Third International".

Gramsci went along for a while with early Stalinism. Maybe he did so because he could not yet see the issues clearly, did not want to be evicted and politically marginalised on grounds he was not sure of, and so could see no other choice. "I don't know yet" was not a permissible stance in the Comintern of 1926. "The authority of the Central Committee between one congress and another", he obediently wrote, "must never be placed under discussion... the party wants to achieve a maximum of collective leadership and will not allow any individual, whatever his value, to oppose himself to the party".

Trotsky was, surely, much sharper and clearer about Stalinism than Gramsci ever was.

1930 would show that, even if for one reason or another some attitudes to Trotsky "stuck" from 1926, Gramsci never went over to Stalinism. His *Prison Notebooks* argue for an open, intellectually-alive revolutionary socialist party.

Both Gramsci and Trotsky emphasised, thought about, and wrote about the question of the revolutionary socialist party much more than other Marxists of their epoch.

"If the theoretical structure of the political economy of Marxism rests entirely upon the conception of value as materialised labour", wrote Trotsky, "the revolutionary policy of Marxism rests upon the conception of the party as the vanguard of the proletariat" [75]. (The word "vanguard" then had none of the militarist connotations brought to it by decades of Stalinism. In the 1870s the Jura anarchists had entitled one of their papers *The Vanguard*. It meant pioneering, forward-looking).

Gramsci wrote that the central question in politics was "developing the concept of hegemony — as has been done in practice in the development of the theory of the political party..." [76]; and that "the protagonist of the new Prince [the "hegemonic apparatus" of organisations, alliances, and activities that could enable the working class to vanquish capitalism] could... only be the political party".

We must beware of anachronism. Neither of them was concerned to dispute the view, common today after the disorienting work of Stalinism, that it could make sense to be a revolutionary-socialist activist but organise only on the trade-union or campaign level and not on that of revolutionary-socialist party-building. That stance would have seemed to them too nonsensical to argue with. Socialist revolution is an aim which requires organised collective activity to bring it about. To think that you can be a serious revolutionary socialist and not organised into a socialist group is as foolish as thinking that instead of organised strike action you can make do with individual workers taking odd days off in random fashion.

They knew of activists who claimed that their organisations were not really "parties", but considered that just a verbal foible.

Gramsci: "Parties may present themselves under the most diverse names, even calling themselves the anti-party or the 'negation of the parties'; in reality, even the so-called 'individualists' are party men, only they would like to be 'party chiefs' by the grace of God..." [77] Trotsky: "French syndicalism... was and is, in its organisation and theory, likewise a party... [Only] the party of revolutionary syndicalism fears the aversion felt by the French working class for parties as such. Therefore it has not assumed the name of party and has... attempted to have its members... take cover behind the trade unions" [78].

They knew also of sympathisers who were not yet ready to take on the commitment of party membership. This is how Trotsky responded to one of them, Maurice Paz, a French lawyer who thought himself Trotskyist but said his busy law practice ruled out full organised activism:

"I am neither a fanatic nor a sectarian. I can very well understand a person who sympathises with the communist cause without leaving his milieu. Assistance of this sort can be very valuable for us. But it is the assistance of a sympathiser.

"I discussed this question in a letter to my American friends. [Max] Eastman had written to me, without mincing words himself, that such was his personal situation. He designates himself a 'fellow-traveller', does not aspire, in his own words, to any leading role in the movement of the Opposition, and is content to assist it. He does translations, he has turned over his copyrights... etc. And why? Because he cannot give himself entirely to the movement. And he has acted correctly. If you don't want to enter the lists, wait quietly, keep a friendly neutrality" [79].

The question for both Gramsci and Trotsky was not whether to work to build a revolutionary-socialist party, but what sort of party, and how.

Both had led mass parties. Trotsky then had to go through a period of working with small nuclei. He did what was necessary. "The different strata of the mass mature at different times. The struggle for the 'maturing' of the mass begins with a minority, with a 'sect', with a vanguard.

There is not and cannot be any other road in history" [80].

Gramsci, in a passage in the *Prison Notebooks* where he appears to be thinking about the risk of fascist repression pulverising his party, also saw the building of a clearly-defined and educated activist core as primary: "This element is endowed with... the power of innovation (innovation, be it understood, in a certain direction, according to certain lines of force, certain perspectives, even certain premises)... This element [could not] form the party alone; however, it could do so more than the first element considered [i.e. the eventual relatively-loose mass membership]... The existence of a united group of generals who agree among themselves and have common aims soon creates an army even where none exists... The criteria by which the [activist core] should be judged are to be sought 1. in what it actually does; 2. in what provision it makes for the eventuality of its own destruction... the preparation of... successors" [81].

There is nothing in Gramsci's writings comparable to Trotsky's explanation, in *Lessons of October* that "a party crisis is inevitable in the transition from preparatory revolutionary activity to the immediate struggle for power. Generally speaking, crises arise in the party at every serious turn in the party's course..." [82] — from which it follows that the party has to develop a breadth of education and pluralism of cadre to allow for rapid shifts in balance and in leadership.

But some questions were studied more by Gramsci than by Trotsky. In 1922 Trotsky had argued for revolutionary-socialist parties relearning "prosaic... organisational-agitational-educational work", and for "criticism, self-criticism, and control" to stop the resulting inevitable and even proper conservatism of "habits and methods of work" becoming noxious. Trotsky left much to develop on what that "criticism, self-criticism, and control" in "prosaic" work would mean.

He explained the difference between a transitional-demand approach, and that of the old minimum/maximum programme scheme of the pre-1914 Marxists; but the overwhelming focus of Trotsky's writings from 1917 to 1940, was on sketching how a Marxist organisation (and, from the late 20s, a small Marxist organisation) could fluidify a miscongealed labour movement in acute crises. Many of his explanations of transitional demands were closely interwoven with pictures of acute crisis, and difficult to unweave for use in other times.

Explosions and catastrophes followed fast on each other. From the early 1930s, Trotsky was convinced both that capitalism was in intractable agony, and that the USSR was so acutely unstable that it could be assessed only as a temporary concatenation of elements bound to fly apart, one way or another, very soon. All that was for good reason, but "one-sided".

Gramsci, stuck in prison, developed a longer-term focus on processes of preparation. "The decisive element in every situation is the permanently organised and long-prepared force which can be put into the field when it is judged that a situation is favourable (and it can be favourable only in so far as such a force exists, and is full of fighting spirit). Therefore the essential task is that of systematically and patiently ensuring that this force is formed, developed, and rendered ever more homogeneous, compact, and self-aware" [22].

What were the necessary elements of "criticism, self-criticism, and control" in that "systematic and patient" activity? Gramsci discussed philosophy and perspectives. There was a drift in the pre-1914 Marxist movement — by no means universal, but eventually dominant — to split perspectives into two levels. On one level, capitalism would move forward economically, creating larger and more concentrated working classes and bringing on itself worse and worse crises. On another, the educational and organisational work of the socialists, instructing workers in the truths derived from statistical observation of economic development, would make the labour movement stronger. Socialist revolution would come when the two lines met in a definitive capitalist crisis and a majority-supported socialist movement.

Gramsci: "In politics the assumption of the law of statistics as an essential law operating of necessity is not only a scientific error but becomes a practical error in action... Political action tends precisely to rouse the masses from passivity, in other words to destroy the law of large numbers. So how can that law be considered a law of sociology?..." [19]

With a big revolutionary party, "knowledge... on the part of the leaders is no longer the product of hunches backed up by the identification of statistical laws, which leaders then translate into ideas and words-as-force... Rather it is acquired by the collective organism through 'active and conscious co-participation', through 'compassionality', through experience of immediate particulars, through a system which one could call 'living philology'..." ["philology" is the study of how languages or words develop historically] [83].

"Only to the extent to which the objective aspect of prediction is linked to a programme does it acquire its objectivity: 1. because strong passions are necessary to sharpen the intellect and help make intuition more penetrating; 2. because reality is a product of the application of human will to the society of things... therefore if one excludes all voluntarist elements, or if it is only other people's wills whose intervention one reckons as an objective element in the general interplay of forces, one mutilates reality itself" [84].

As he showed in his writings on schooling, Gramsci was not a naive enthusiast of learning-by-doing. He recognised the necessity of formal "instruction". But he integrated it as an element within a "philosophy of praxis" which, even if it has serious lacunae, is far more enlightening than what became the Stalinist scheme of a "Marxist philosophy" based on alleged iron laws of natural development.

Gramsci was developing themes first sketched by Antonio Labriola, a late 19th century philosopher who gradually, as a maverick on the fringes of the socialist movement, developed a supple and imaginative version of Marxism as "philosophy of practice". (Trotsky, in his autobiography, cited Labriola as his own first teacher in Marxist method; but thereafter Trotsky wrote about philosophy only when he felt forced to by urgent constraints of polemic).

Teaching, so Labriola had argued, is "an activity which generates another activity". Gramsci reconceptualised the way in which a revolutionary socialist party must strive to educate the working class as the activity of a collective "democratic philosopher" and "permanently active persuader".

He argued that political polemic must proceed differently from military battle, in which wisdom is to seek the opposition's weakest points. "On the ideological front... the defeat of the auxiliaries and the minor hangers-on is of all but negligible importance. It is necessary to engage battle with the most eminent of one's adversaries... if the end proposed is that of raising the tone and intellectual level of one's followers and not just... of creating a desert around oneself by all means possible" [85].

Where the Catholic church had kept together learned people and a mass following by "imposing an iron discipline on the intellectuals", the socialist movement must avoid "restricting scientific activity" and instead organise a continual process of intellectual interchange and levelling-up [86].

Much of Trotsky's attention was focused on frantic short-term alternatives of revolution and catastrophe. The pre-1914 Marxist movement had tended to see capitalist development as linear evolution. Gramsci developed another concept, "passive revolution", or "revolution/restoration", of processes in which a ruling class extends itself and reshapes society by absorbing or decapitating other elements.

Trotsky had discussed this sort of possibility of "reactionary progress" in earlier writings. "Theoretically, to be sure, even a new chapter of a general capitalist progress in the most powerful, ruling, and leading countries is not excluded. But for this, capitalism would... have to strangle the proletarian revolution for a long time; it would have to enslave China completely, overthrow the Soviet republic, and so forth" [87].

By 1938, under the pressure of events, Trotsky had drifted into a too-absolute "negativism" about capitalism, which he saw as able only to descend deeper into chaos. In parallel, his urgent search for revolutionary recompositions of the labour movement had drifted into an unrealistic overestimation of the possibilities for small socialist groups to find ways to "switch the points" (as he once put it) for the "train" of an already-existing but misled socialist workers' movement.

In some passages of the Transitional Programme, therefore, as in the famous one about the "crisis of humanity" being "reduced to the crisis of leadership", the prospect of revolution appears in almost mystical form, as a sudden apocalyptic coming-together of elemental mass working-class rage and a revolutionary leadership prepared by pure willpower. "The harsh and tragic dialectic of our epoch is working in our favour. Brought to the extreme pitch of exasperation and indignation, the masses will find no other leadership than that offered to them by the Fourth International" [88].

Perhaps Trotsky had no choice but to make this "error", or else resign himself to defeatism in a situation where the labour movement faced dramatic short-term choices to mobilise for revolution, or be crushed. For sure, abstracted, crudified, and dogmatised versions of his vision would contribute to much sectarian posturing in the decades that followed. They would overwhelm Trotsky's subtler explanations:

"Agitation is not only the means of communicating to the masses this or that slogan, calling the masses to action, etc. For a party, agitation is also a means of lending an ear to the masses, of sounding out its moods and thoughts, and reaching this or another decision in accordance with the results. Only the Stalinists have transformed agitation into a noisy monologue. For the Marxists, the Leninists, agitation is always a dialogue with the masses. But in order that this dialogue gives the necessary results, the party must estimate correctly the general situation within the country and outline the general course of the immediate struggle. By means of agitation and probing the masses, the party must bring into its concepts the necessary corrections and exactitude..." [89]

Against the sectarian posturing — not Trotsky's, but in a certain sense Trotskyist — Gramsci has much to teach us. The activity of a revolutionary socialist party, he explained, has to be something much more than juxtaposing itself, with a supposedly "finished programme", to elemental revolt. It is a process of continual dialogue, intervention, reorganisation, readjustment, and transformation both of the mass labour movement and of the party itself.

In an economistic, barebones-Marxist scheme, he wrote, everything "appears as a moralistic accusation of duplicity and bad faith, or.... of naivety and stupidity. Thus the political struggle is reduced to a series of personal affairs between on the one hand those with the genie in the lamp who know everything and on the other those who are fooled by their own leaders but are so incurably thick that they refuse to believe it".

Thinking is often warped by a belief in "objective laws of historical development similar in kind to natural laws, together with a belief in a predetermined teleology like that of a religion: since favourable conditions are inevitably going to appear, and since these, in a rather mysterious way, will bring about palingenetic events [regenerating events, i.e., revolutions], it is evident that any deliberate initiative tending to predispose and plan these conditions is not only useless but even harmful. Side by side with these fatalistic beliefs however, there exists the tendency 'thereafter' to rely blindly and indiscriminately on the regulatory properties of armed conflict...

"In such modes of thinking, no account is taken of the 'time' factor, nor in the last analysis even of 'economics'. For there is no understanding of the fact that mass ideological factors always lag behind mass economic phenomena, and that therefore, at certain moments, the automatic thrust due to the economic factor is slowed down, obstructed or even momentarily broken by traditional ideological elements — hence there must be a conscious, planned struggle to ensure that the exigencies of the economic position of the masses, which may conflict with the traditional leadership's policies, are understood. An appropriate political initiative is always necessary to liberate the economic thrust from the dead weight of traditional policies..." [90].

A Gramsci glossary

Martin Thomas

CAESARISM. By Caesarism Gramsci meant much the same as other Marxists have meant by Bonapartism. Quintin Hoare (SPN p.206) argues that Gramsci's "Caesarism" was broader than other Marxists' "Bonapartism", but I read Gramsci more as considering gradations of Caesarism as well as full Caesarism (SPN p.220).

CIVIL SOCIETY. Gramsci uses the word "State" in two different senses (and explains that he is doing that). Sometimes he uses "state" to mean government in the narrow sense, which he also calls "political society". Sometimes he uses it to mean the "integral State", the whole machinery of rule and hegemony of the ruling class: "State = political society + civil society". Sometimes he makes a contrast, state vs. civil society; sometimes he apparently equates state and civil society.

The fact that Gramsci was writing with such examples in mind as fascist Italy (and a Europe where fascism was advancing), or the Stalinising USSR, may explain why Gramsci seems to overestimate the seamlessness and coherence of the "integral State" ("political society + civil society").

It may also explain why Gramsci's discussions of "the integral state" appear to show a "functionalist" or "instrumentalist" bias, an assumption that because these things serve the ruling class therefore they correspond to what the ruling class wants them to do.

"A liberal, democratic regime", wrote Gramsci, would be necessary for "the great intellectuals" to be able to animate civil hegemony with some leeway from the government (he was commenting on an argument by Croce: SPN p.271). In "illiberal structures of government", he wrote, "civil society merges with political society" (Buttigieg vol.3 p.48).

Gramsci came to see fascism as the dominant political form in Europe for his day. "In the present epoch, the war of movement took place politically from March 1917 to March 1921: this was followed by a war of position whose representative — both practical (for Italy) and ideological (for

Europe) — is fascism" (SPN p.120). In his Prison Notebooks he cannot be taken as writing just about current events, but Gramsci did not consider Italian fascism a quirk or exception for his epoch. It is wrong to read the notebooks (as they are sometimes read) as focused on examining patterns of bourgeois-democratic societies in contrast to authoritarian regimes like Tsarist Russia. The notebooks do discuss denser networks of "civil society" typical of developed bourgeois democracies. But they discuss those denser networks usually with fascist society in mind. When we relate Gramsci's discussion to the relatively stable bourgeois democracies of Western Europe in recent decades, we must always keep in our mind that Gramsci has in his mind a different backdrop.

Gramsci refers to "civil society" as a set of private associations and networks. To that extent his usage is similar to modern journalistic and academic usage. Gramsci is concerned mostly with political parties, newspapers, schools, etc., and suggests (with fascist Italy in mind) that the dominant civil-society elements operate to "trickle down" consent to ruling-class power. Modern academic and journalistic usage looks more to NGOs, charities, think-tanks, pressure groups, etc., and sees them mostly as operating the other way round, providing channels for citizens' concerns to "trickle up" into the public sphere.

As Quintin Hoare points out (SPN p.208), Gramsci does not often talk of the economic structure as a constituent of civil society. The passage which Hoare cites as Gramsci (by way of exception) including economic structure within civil society I read as saying that civil society works to conform social psychology to the demands of the economic structure.

In a passage where Gramsci described the way he used the term "civil society" as distinct from how others used it, he equated his usage with Hegel's. Yet, in understating or neglecting economic structure as a constituent of civil society, in emphasising voluntary associations as vehicles of consent contrasted with the state as vehicle of coercion, Gramsci's usage was a bit different from Hegel's.

"A distinction must be made between civil society as understood by Hegel, and as often used in these notes (i.e. in the sense of political and cultural hegemony of a social group over the entire society, as ethical content of the State), and on the other hand civil society in the sense in which it is understood by Catholics, for whom civil society is instead political society of the State, in contrast with the society of family and that of the Church". (Quoted in SPN, p.208).

Hegel's ideas would have come to Gramsci by way of Benedetto

Croce, the foremost liberal (and one-time Marxist) philosopher of the time in Italy, who had written a book on Hegel.

For Hegel (*Philosophy of Right*, §182): "Civil society is the stage of difference which intervenes between the family and the state, even if its formation follows later in time than that of the state... The creation of civil society is the achievement of the modern world which has for the first time given all determinations of the Idea their due... The whole sphere of civil society is the territory of mediation where there is free play for every idiosyncrasy, every talent, every accident of birth and fortune, and where waves of every passion gush forth, regulated only by reason glinting through them..."

Civil society was the set of economic, legal, and corporate institutions which mediated the difficulties of the market and sustained the state, though the state was the primary creative, consent-making, force.

In modern academic and journalistic discussion, "civil society" means institutions outside the market and the state (and, implicitly, outside the family too). They are seen not as a dimension of ruling-class rule, and not very much as regulators of the market, but as a counterweight to the state, and pivotal in making bourgeois democracy more than periodic vote-counting. Usually, though without much explanation, the focus is on NGOs, charities, and so on, and especially on the spectrum of "civil society" operating through grants, offices, paid staff, and so on. As Steven Rathgeb Smith notes, critically (*Oxford Handbook of Civil Society*, ed. Michael Edwards, 2011, p.34), the "typology has tended to minimise the importance of... the arts, sports and recreation, and social clubs... Trade unions also tend to be excluded from consideration".

Historically, the term has had different meanings. (See "Aux origines de la société civile", by Raffaele Laudani, *Le Monde diplomatique*, September 2012).

For Adam Ferguson, in his *Essay on the History of Civil Society* (1767), "civil" was an attribute which society as a whole would have or not have. Ferguson was concerned with the modes by which society could be "civil" despite the pullulating rivalries of the burgeoning capitalist market and capitalist cities, in which the old, fixed social ties of rank and place were dissolved.

Acquisitive individuals "would enter, if not restrained by the laws of civil society, on a scene of violence or meanness, which would exhibit our species, by turns, under an aspect more terrible and odious, or more vile and contemptible, than that of any animal which inherits the earth". "In a commercial state... man is sometimes found a detached and solitary being: he has found an object which sets him in competition with his fellow-creatures, and he deals with them as he does with his cattle and his soil, for the sake of the profits they bring". So statesmen would find "those public establishments which tend to keep the peace of society, a respite from foreign wars, and a relief from domestic disorders. They learn to decide every contest without tumult, and to secure, by the authority of law, every citizen in the possession of his personal rights. In this condition, to which thriving nations aspire, and which they in some measure attain, mankind having laid the basis of safety, proceed to erect a superstructure suitable to their views.

"The desire of lucre is the great motive to injuries: law therefore has a principal reference to property". It must give security to, but not cripple, bourgeois enterprise. "The object in commerce is to make the individual rich; the more he gains for himself, the more he augments the wealth of his country. If a protection be required, it must be granted; if crimes and frauds be committed, they must be repressed; and government can pretend to no more".

His contemporary Adam Smith (*The Wealth of Nations*, 1776) seconded this view: "The acquisition of valuable and extensive [and, he might have added, mobile] property, therefore, necessarily requires the establishment of civil government. Where there is no property, or at least none that exceeds the value of two or three days labour, civil government is not so necessary".

For such writers, "the sphere of private property... was a sphere of egoism and self-interest, where people pursue their own aims regardless of the welfare of others and use others simply as a means to their own private welfare... An authority had to be established... which would reconcile the contradictions and embody [the] social, moral, or rational aspect of human existence" (Robert Fine, *Democracy and the Rule of Law*, Pluto 1984, p.12).

Hegel, in his *Philosophy of Right* (1820), began to categorise "civil society" as an element in society distinct from the state, rather than a sort of society. He did it by building directly on the ideas of Ferguson and Smith. For Hegel, "civil society" was the complex of provisions instituted by the state to mediate between itself and the family households.

"The protection of property by the administration of justice" was fundamental to civil society, but civil society should also include "provision against possible mischances, and care for the particular interest as a common interest... general arrangements for education". With a thought that would inform Croce, whom Gramsci studied closely, Hegel described civil society as "the world of ethical appearance".

That this was a discussion of a particular society, based on market economy and bourgeois enterprise, was made explicit by Hegel in the fact that the German term he used for "civil society", "bürgerliche Gesellschaft", also and equally means "bourgeois society".

Marx did not develop Hegel's train of thought further, but rather turned off at a different angle. For Hegel, as for Ferguson and Smith, the problem of "civil society" was how to adjust institutions so that society could thrive and control the rapacity of bourgeois market economy, which had developed naturally and was "the end of history" in economic structures.

In his *Preface to his Contribution to the Critique of Political Economy* (1859), Marx wrote of: "... the material conditions of life, the totality of which Hegel, following the example of English [in fact, Scottish] and French thinkers of the eighteenth century, embraces within the term 'civil society'... the anatomy of this civil society, however, has to be sought in political economy".

For Marx, like Hegel, civil society was bourgeois society. For Marx, unlike Hegel, civil society was not the creation of the state, but the base that shaped it. The economic structure was not only part of civil society, but the basis of its anatomy. Marx wanted not to harmonise social institutions with the basis, but to identify the contradictions within the basis which would result in society being revolutionarily transformed by an element within that basis, the working class.

Meanwhile, another strand feeding into modern discussions of "civil society" had been formulated by the conservative Edmund Burke. Railing against all comprehensive social change, such as executed by the French Revolution, he wrote: "To be attached to the subdivision, to love the little platoon we belong to in society, is the first principle (the germ as it were) of public affections. It is the first link in the series by which we proceed towards a love to our country" (*Reflections on the Revolution in France*, 1790). Like Hegel, though from a different angle, he saw a need for intermediary institutions to stabilise a society otherwise starkly divided between a remote state and atomised individuals.

The same idea was developed in a different mode by the liberal Alexis de Tocqueville in *Democracy in America* (1835-40). "Americans of all ages, conditions, and all dispositions constantly unite together. Not only do they have commercial and industrial associations... but also a thousand other kinds, religious, moral, serious, futile, very general and very specialised, large and small... In democratic nations, associations must take the place of those powerful individuals who have been swept away by the equality of social conditions".

For Tocqueville, this multitude of associations was the foundation of liberal bourgeois democracy.

The modern academic and journalistic use of the term "civil society" is closer to Tocqueville than to any other predecessor, though Tocqueville's concern was mainly with groups run by their memberships. As Theda Skocpol notes, in the USA since the 1970s and 80s many "civil society" groups "are not membership groups at all. Many others are staff-centred associations... that recruit most supporters individually via the mail or media messages" (*Oxford Handbook of Civil Society*, ed. Michael Edwards, 2011, p.112).

In a turnabout from the 18th century usage, "civil society" has come to be seen as the element which civilises the state (and the capitalist market), rather than the state being the major element which civilises civil society (dominated by the capitalist market).

Marx did not use the term "civil society" for the spread of voluntary associations in bourgeois society; but he did see the spread of association, among the working class, as the engine for changing "civil society".

In the Communist Manifesto, Marx described the following evolution of associations. "The workers begin to form combinations (trade unions) against the bourgeois... This union is helped on by the improved means of communication that are created by modern industry... The organisation of the proletarians into a class, and consequently into a political party...

"The bourgeoisie... sees itself [in its political clashes] compelled to appeal to the proletariat... to drag it into the political arena. The bourgeoisie itself, therefore, supplies the proletariat with its own elements of political and general education.... Sections of the ruling classes are... precipitated into the proletariat... supply the proletariat with fresh elements of enlightenment and progress... A portion of the bourgeois ideologists... goes over to the proletariat..."

Rather than seeing voluntary associations primarily as trenches and fortresses of bourgeois power, Marx reckoned even bourgeois "civil society" associations might contribute to working-class ferment. The more "civil society" (in the Tocqueville sense), the more trade unions, the more working-class associations of all sorts, the better communications, the more schools and universities, the more political ferment, etc., the stronger the working class, at least potentially. In that sense his perception had more in common with the modern usage than with Hegel or with Gramsci. Marx's focus was on trade unions and working-class parties, not NGO operations centred on paid staff working in an office financed by grants, or charities.

To translate Gramsci's discussion of "civil society" into a left-wing politics based on building up NGOs and think-tanks is to make nonsense of it. He saw the building of a revolutionary socialist workers' party as central to developing a "hegemonic apparatus" of the working class within civil society.

What is distinctive about Gramsci is not a specially clear or useful definition of "civil society", but the explicit argument that a revolutionary socialist party must wage an ideological struggle on every front, and on a level adequate to counter the best and sharpest thinkers of the bourgeoisie. Launching his paper *Ordine Nuovo* in 1919, he wrote: "the journal should encourage the complete development of one's mental capacities for a higher and fuller life, richer in harmony and ideological aims..." He pursued the same theme in the Notebooks.

On one level, the idea was not new. Even pre-Marxist socialists, like the Owenites, had concerned themselves with education and enlightenment on many fronts. The German Social-Democratic Party, and the German Communist Party after it, ran a rich range of "cultural" activities. Lenin in *What Is To Be Done?* argued for socialist journalism to expose oppression on every front, including those which did not directly concern the working class.

But Gramsci elaborated. A revolutionary socialist party, aiming to change the world totally, must roll out a world-view capable of challenging today's rulers, at least in outline, on every front, not just on the bottom-line economic and political questions.

Gramsci also understood some necessary limitations. He contributed a chapter to Trotsky's *Literature and Revolution,* and will have understood Trotsky's argument there that bourgeois culture can only be superseded by absorbing its best contributions and moving on to a classless culture, not by counterposing a "proletarian culture" which is improvised amidst the poverty and the educationally-starved situation of an exploited class and is therefore necessarily the more or less arbitrary invention of a few over-confident ideologues.

On *Ordine Nuovo*, rather than insisting that the paper follow a strictly combative line on cultural issues, Gramsci invited a self-proclaimed liberal, Piero Gobetti, to write the paper's theatre reviews.

There may be passages in the Notebooks where Gramsci oversteps the necessary qualifications in his attempt to depict the triumphant revolutionary socialist party as the carrier of a complete world-view. But that is another issue.

How does the question of "civil society" (in the Tocqueville sense) stand today?

In Western Europe, and not only in Western Europe, in let's say the 1940s, the big elements of Tocquevillian civil society were the unions, the political parties, the press, the churches, and schools and universities.

Some of those elements have faded. The mainstream bourgeois political parties have faded. The Tory party in Britain had 2.8 million members in 1953 — three times as many individual members as the Labour Party had at its peak, around the same time — and they were organised in a web of Conservative Clubs and Associations, active in their own way. Now it has maybe 150,000 members, with an average age of around 64. Despite the Tories doing well electorally, they have fewer members even than the much-shrunken Labour Party. Their membership has halved under David Cameron's apparently-successful leadership.

The Liberal party had nearly 300,000 members in the 1960s, when they had only between six and nine MPs and had had no more than nine since 1950; today the Liberal Democrats have only 40-odd thousand, despite at one point in the run-up to the 2010 election running higher in the polls than both Tories and Labour.

Union membership has mostly declined since the early 1980s. The churches have shrunk, too. Press circulation has shrunk. It has been replaced only partly by TV viewing.

In the early 1960s, there was much discussion about this in Britain. Writers argued that we were in a new age of systematic "apathy", "end of ideology", "instrumental" attitudes, atomisation, and so on. Instead of participating in civil society, people were commuting to work, watching television, going on package holidays, and buying more and more fridges, washing machines, televisions, cars, etc.

The theorists of the early 1960s would find as early as 1968 that their extrapolation of ever-increasing apathy was wrong. And they underestimated the residual hegemonic power of the old political and trade-union apparatuses.

Today there is less atomisation. Schooling, which despite the rise of online learning is still mostly face-to-face, has expanded hugely. Social media, through which people are "networked" but not exactly organised, have expanded even more.

In the USA, people spend an average of 14 hours a month — or 20 hours a month for people aged 18-34 — on networking over social media. They overwhelmingly communicate with people they also know in real life, or with whom they are put in touch by mutual friends. When asked to describe how they feel after time spent networking, the words they by far most often choose are "connected" and "informed". Some choose the word "indifferent", but the numbers choosing the terms "excited" or "energised" are not very far behind. (*Nielsen Social Media Report* 2012).

We need to reckon with these trends. But can this area of "civil society" be an alternative to the unions and the old workers' movement in finding points of leverage for socialist struggle? Evidently as Marxists we must find points of leverage for socialist struggle within bourgeois civil society as it exists (even if in the short term the leverage is limited, and it takes much effort to organise even small elements of struggle) — or else we become just utopians and peddlers of blueprints.

Elsewhere (www.workersliberty.org/tweet) I have argued that this expansion of wide, loose networking in civil society cannot be seen not a substitute for the strong organised networking which the working class needs to fight and to win. It is rather one of the terrains to be built on for assembling (as fast as we can, as patiently as we must) elements for that organisation — on somewhat the same level as the older environment of smaller but tighter networks (neighbours, connections made through particular cafes or pubs, churches) was also a background terrain but not a substitute.

The "Arab Spring" of 2011, after the first eruption of loosely-networked protest toppled the dictators, was then progressively confiscated by the strong organised networks of the Islamists. Possibilities are not closed off, but the left and the worker activists in Egypt and Tunisia face big difficulties in building strong-enough alternatives. "Networking" is not a substitute for organisation.

COERCION AND CONSENT. Ruling classes, says Gramsci, rule not only through the machinery of government (coercion); they also lead in society and win consent through political parties, media, school systems, etc.

Gramsci formulates this thought many times in the Prison Notebooks, and sometimes cites "pairs" (force-consent, authority-hegemony, political society-civil society, etc.: e.g. SPN p.169) as if all these pairs are neat divisions of reality into two boxes, and equivalent ways of saying the same thing (like fish-chips, seafood-potatoes, poisson-frites, etc.)

However, this is misleading. Gramsci writes that political society (the machinery of government) and civil society are only aspects of a whole. "The distinction [between political society and civil society] is purely methodological and not organic; in concrete historical life, political society and civil society are a single entity" (Buttigieg vol.2 p.182). It may be more accurate to see political society and civil society as different strands of class activity, going on interdependently and both over a swathe of social life, than as different areas of social life.

Gramsci also writes that there are forms of power other than coercion and consent. "Between consent and force stands corruption/fraud (which is characteristic of certain situations when it is hard to exercise the hegemonic function, and when the use of force is too risky). This consists in procuring the demoralisation and paralysis of the antagonist (or antagonists) by buying its leaders... in order to sow disarray and confusion in his ranks..." (SPN p.80).

Even so, it can be objected that Gramsci neglects the "dull compulsion of economic relations" and the embedded "illusions created by competition" and "commodity fetishism" of which Marx wrote in *Capital*; and that he also neglects the sort of "dull compulsion of political relations" established by a developed bourgeois democracy above and beyond whatever measure of "consent" the various leading parties may get (or may not get, as in Italy in 1994).

It can also be objected that usual interpretations of Gramsci, and maybe even Gramsci himself, mislead us by pairing coercion with political society and consent with civil society.

Edward Said's usage in *Orientalism* is an example. "Gramsci has made the useful analytic distinction between civil and political society in which the former is made up of voluntary (or at least rational and non-coercive) affiliations like schools, families, and unions, the latter of state institutions (the army, the police, the central bureaucracy) whose role in the polity is direct domination" (p.6).

The army and the police are armed. They shoot people or lock them up for long periods, and schoolteachers, fathers, and workplace bosses do not. The army and the police are the bourgeoisie's reserve forces of coercion.

However, nagging doubts made Said insert a parenthesis, "or at least rational and non-coercive"; and the parenthesis is inadequate. Everyday coercion of working-class people in even minimally bourgeois-democratic societies is vastly more by schoolteachers, parents, workplace bosses, private security guards, and bailiffs than directly by cops or soldiers. That everyday coercion makes impositions, every day, which have "consent", if at all, only in the most grudging "no option but to put up with it" sense.

The police, by contrast, even if unpopular, rely heavily on everyday deference rather than explicit violence to regulate people. Police in the US are surely more directly coercive than in European societies, for example, but US figures find that "nearly 45 million people had face-to-face contact with police over a 12-month period and that approximately one percent, or about 500,000 of these persons, were subjected to use of force or threat of force" (*Use of Force by Police: overview of national and local data*, US Department of Justice, 1999, p.3). Cops' assaults on picket lines and demonstrations are significant components of bourgeois class rule, but are one element in a complex dominated by a certain sort of "consent".

The police also, more or less, operate a system of laws which is regulated by democratically-elected assemblies and which prevails mostly through a form of consent rather than crude coercion. Socialists rightly and frequently say "better to break the law than break the poor", but we do so to make a case with working-class people who, most of the time, think that breaking the law is undesirable and requires special justification.

Workplace bosses, by contrast, often operate impositions which are accepted by workers with no "consent" beyond a feeling that economic coercion gives them no choice but to submit.

The pairing consent-civil, coercion-political, is thus misleading. So is the omission of workplaces from the catalogue of institutions of bourgeois rule. Perry Anderson's point, discussed elsewhere in these pages, that the engineering of consent in bourgeois-democratic societies operates in important part through "political society" rather than "civil society", is confirmed.

Gramsci does not, by emphasising the problem of consent, intend for revolutionary socialists to replace sharp class struggle by patient nudging of public opinion. He writes that forms of German ideological predominance in Europe before 1914, including the predominance in the socialist parties in many countries of the German SPD's Marxist doctrine, were "merely a phenomenon of abstract cultural influence" because they lacked "organic or disciplinary bonds". "Abstract cultural influence" was no substitute for "real activity" (SPN p.188).

COHERENCE: with Gramsci, this is to do with coherence between theory and practice, as well as coherence within theory. According to Peter Thomas, it "can be regarded as one of the 'keywords' of the conceptual architecture of the Prison Notebooks... traversing the border between the strictly philosophical and the strictly political... Gramsci deploys the concept of coherence precisely as a synonym for... the 'union of theory and practice' and more particularly for... 'union of Marxist theory and the workers' movement'." (*The Gramscian Moment*, pp.364-5)

DUAL PERSPECTIVE. Gramsci's discussion takes as its starting point ideas from the Fifth Congress of the Comintern (June-July 1924) which were in fact a fudge rather than a valuable theoretical innovation.

Quintin Hoare explains: "The Congress followed a long series of defeats for the revolution internationally, culminating in the German October of 1923. Zinoviev... was anxious to present... the German revolution as still being on the cards in the immediate future. Trotsky and Radek were arguing that [the defeat in Germany had been serious and far-reaching and] the European bourgeoisie was moving in the direction of a [temporary] 'labourist' resolution of its post-war political crisis, witness events in England and France".

There was some polemic against Trotsky as being soft on social democracy, but Stalin and Zinoviev — who was then allied with Stalin, and president of the Comintern — did not yet feel confident enough to dispute Trotsky head-on.

"Under Zinoviev's guidance, the Congress in effect adopted a compromise solution, allowing both for the imminence of revolution and for a generalisation of the 'labourist' solution... The Theses... stated: 'The whole situation is such that two perspectives are open: (a) a possible slow and prolonged development of the proletarian revolution, and (b) on the other hand... the solution in one country or another may come in the not distant future'." (SPN p.169).

It was a fudge. Gramsci didn't see it that way, and in any case seized on this formula, which at least allowed for some complexity in developments, against the Stalinist doctrine of the "Third Period" in which every crisis was deemed to lead directly towards workers' revolution.

In discussions with other communist prisoners at Turi, Gramsci spoke (so Hoare reports) "of the 'two perspectives'... He said that of the two, the more likely was that of some form of transitional stage intervening between the fall of fascism amid the dictatorship of the proletariat, and that the party's tactics should take this into account".

Maybe Gramsci was influenced there by Trotsky's similar argument: "Expectations that Fascism, becoming steadily more and more intensified, will lead to the uprising of the proletariat, have not been justified by experience, and by no means all of us shared these expectations" (June 1924).

In the Notebooks, Gramsci discusses the "dual perspective" in what at first sight seems an entirely different way: as a matter of dual levels in the revolutionary organisation's activity rather than of expectations allowing for two possible developments in the broad political situation.

"Another point which needs to be defined and developed is the 'dual perspective' in political action and in national life. The dual perspective can present itself on various levels, from the most elementary to the most complex; but these can all theoretically be reduced to two fundamental levels... of force and of consent, authority and hegemony, violence and civilisation... of agitation and of propaganda, of tactics and of strategy, etc."

In periods of "slow development" (as the Fifth Congress had it) the revolutionary party would chiefly be concerned with propaganda; with incremental tactics; with "civilisation" in the sense of the gradual education of its own forces and of the working class and also of small battles which win more "civilised" conditions for workers within capitalism; with gradually building up support (consent, hegemony).

In a revolutionary crisis, tasks connected with force, authority, violence, strategy, and agitation would be foremost. (The traditional Marxist usage on "propaganda" and "agitation" is that "propaganda" is about longer-term educational activity, explaining a large complex of ideas to a relatively small audience, and "agitation" is about explaining one or a few ideas to a larger audience on the basis of current events which give those ideas a wider reach. "Propaganda", then, meant education or enlightenment, without the connotations of deception and manipulation which the word acquired in later decades).

Gramsci argued that these two levels should not be separated, or seen as coming in distinct stages, with the activities to do with "force" and so on coming only after a period of gradually building up "consent". This argument runs counter to any view of Gramsci as having concluded that, not just that steady and low-key tactics were required for the next map-pable period, but also that only such tactics would ever be viable in Western Europe. And despite Gramsci's polemics against Rosa Luxemburg, the argument here is very similar to Rosa Luxemburg's in *The Mass Strike*.

"Some have reduced the theory of the 'dual perspective' to something trivial and banal, to nothing but two forms of 'immediacy' which succeed each other mechanically in time, with greater or less 'proximity'. In actual fact, it often happens that the more the first 'perspective' is 'immediate' and elementary, the more the second has to be 'distant' (not in time, but as a dialectical relation), complex and ambitious.

"In other words, it may happen as in human life, that the more an individual is compelled to defend his own immediate physical existence, the more will he uphold and identify with the highest values of civilisation and of humanity, in all their complexity" (SPN p.170).

These arguments by Gramsci do not answer the points made by Trotsky and the Left Opposition in 1923-4. The Left Opposition's forecast was much more specific than just one of "slow development". They were aware that the forecast was only hypothetical and conditional. As Trotsky wrote: "We had in mind only the tendency of development. This did not mean that we were a hundred per cent convinced that things would happen exactly in that way: the tendency of development is one thing, and its living refraction in reality is another thing".

Gramsci also wrote that "relations of forces" should be analysed on three levels (not two) — basic social and economic structure, political organisation and balance, and politico-military relations.

This suggests that the dualities which Gramsci uses in his Notebooks are not about, or not only about, dividing what happens in society into two spheres, but rather about distinguishing, for methodological purposes, what happens into society into simultaneous streams of different time-scales: "the present moment" is a combination of a number of different "present moments" set into those different time-scales.

EAST AND WEST. In 1924 Gramsci wrote against a schematic division of revolutionary socialist strategies into one for the "East" and another for the "West". "Amadeo [Bordiga, another leading figure in the Italian Communist Party]... thinks that the tactic of the [Communist] International reflects the Russian situation, i.e. was born on the terrain of a backward and primitive capitalist civilisation. For him, this tactic is extremely voluntaristic and theatrical, because only with an extreme effort of will was it possible to obtain from the Russian masses a revolutionary action which was not determined by the historical situation...

"[In the West] there exists the historical determinism which was lacking in Russia, and therefore the overriding tasks must be the organisation of the party as an end in itself.

"I think the situation is quite different. Firstly, because the political conception of the Russian communists was formed on an international and not on a national terrain. Secondly, because in central and western Europe the development of capitalism has not only determined the formation of the broad proletarian strata, but also — and as a consequence — has created the higher stratum, the labour aristocracy, with its appendages in the trade-union bureaucracy and the social-democratic groups.

"The determination, which in Russia was direct and drove the masses onto the streets for a revolutionary uprising, in central and western Europe is complicated by all these political superstructures, created by the greater development of capitalism. This makes the action of the masses slower and more prudent, and therefore requires of the revolutionary party a strategy and tactics altogether more complex and long-term than those which were necessary for the Bolsheviks in the period between March and November 1917..." (David Forgacs, ed., *A Gramsci Reader*, 1988, p.130-1).

In a 1926 article, Gramsci further specified another "complication", the greater strength of the states and the ruling classes in Western Europe.

However, better known is a passage from the Prison Notebooks: "A change was necessary from the war of manoeuvre applied victoriously in the East in 1917, to a war of position which was the only possible form in the West... In the East [i.e. in Russia of 1917], the State was everything, civil society was primordial and gelatinous; in the West, there was a proper relationship between State and civil society, and when the State trembled a sturdy structure of civil society was at once revealed. The State was only an outer ditch, behind which there was a powerful system of fortresses and earthworks..." (SPN p.238).

This is wrong. The idea that the state had ever in Russia been "everything", above only a "primordial" and not "sturdy" civil society, is an echo of the idea of the Russian state "hanging in mid-air" which the Russian socialist Pyotr Tkachev argued in the mid-1870s. At the time Frederick Engels showed that the Russian state, on the contrary, had a substantial basis in bourgeois and landowning classes.

By the time of the October 1917 revolution, the old Tsarist state was the very opposite of "everything". It had been smashed by the uprising of February 1917, which drove the police completely off the streets of the cities, destroyed the top commanders' control of the army, and disabled the old machinery of government. What the workers overthrew in October 1917 was a bourgeois semi-state, which had been uneasily coupled with the power of soviets (workers' councils) since February 1917.

The military analogies "war of position" and "war of manoeuvre" do not work well (see "war of position").

Despite what Gramsci had written in his 1924 polemic, it was in February and not in October that there was some "direct determination" which "drove the masses onto the streets for a revolutionary uprising". The February revolution was to a serious extent a surprise attack in a Petersburg where Tsarist power was weak because of the disaffection of the troops stationed there (it was a "surprise" to the workers who over-threw the Tsarist state, too). Bolshevik activity between February and October 1917 was almost entirely a matter of "patiently explaining", as Lenin put it: winning a majority in the soviets. The element of fast-moving manoeuvre was almost trivial. Even on 25-6 October, as Trotsky describes it in his *History of the Russian Revolution*, "demonstrations, street fights, barricades — everything comprised in the usual idea of insurrec-tion — were almost entirely absent".

Middle-class leaders were able to dominate the workers' councils in February 1917, and get them to cede power to the Provisional Government. The middle-class leaders were able to do that precisely because of their strength in "civil society" — in political parties, in the press, etc. If "civil society" in Russia was "gelatinous", that seems a factor conducive to it absorbing working-class assaults rather than being shat-tered by them; in any case Gramsci himself used the same adjective, "gelatinous", to described the "economic and social structure" of his part of the "West", namely Italy.

The evidence of revolutionary working-class upheavals in relatively advanced capitalist countries — Germany 1918-9, Spain 1936-7, France 1968, Portugal 1975 — is not at all that the capitalist state gives way, but then "a sturdy structure of civil society... fortresses and earthworks" saves bourgeois power. The structures of civil society gave way, or were turned around by the working class. (Gramsci himself writes that there had been a "crisis of hegemony" or a loss of ruling-class "civil hegemony" after World War One; or again that "the hegemonic apparatus of the dominant group... disintegrated in every state throughout the world as a result of the [First World] war" — Buttigieg vol. 3 p.211). Yet the state stayed strong enough that the workers could be quelled.

Moreover, as Plekhanov often pointed out in his polemics against the Russian advocates of peasant socialism and of politics for the "East" contrasted to those in the "West", there are many different "Easts" and "Wests".

Italy in Gramsci's day was probably more different from Britain (say) than from Russia. It ranked behind Russia in steel production per head and coal consumption per head; like Russia, it had a few concentrations of advanced, large-scale industry in the midst of a mostly agricultural economy. Agriculture in Italy was mostly as backward and poverty-stricken as in Russia.

Gramsci in his Prison Notebooks discussed at length another "West" — the USA. He saw it (wrongly on the facts, I think) as another country where civil society was underdeveloped, more like Russia in that respect than Western Europe.

Gramsci's comments on East and West have often been used to bolster an idea that revolutionary politics were necessary for socialists in Russia in 1917, but some more gradualist option will work better in more advanced capitalist countries. This is at best a case of picking on weak passages in Notebooks which Gramsci wrote while lacking books and materials to refer to, while in poor health, and while isolated from political and theoretical discussion. Gramsci himself wrote that his notes were fragmentary and provisional, and on some questions "the very opposite of what they asserted will be shown to be the case" (Buttigieg vol.3 p.231).

ECONOMISM. The term "Economism" was first used to name a trend in the Russian Marxist movement around 1899-1901. The "Economists" were bowled over by the success in the mid and late 1890s of leafleting on workplace issues by the underground Marxist circles which previously had mostly been unable to be much more than discussion and self-education groups. They advocated that the Marxists focus their effort more or less entirely on economic issues and for the time being leave to the liberals political issues of the struggle for democracy against Tsarism. Both Lenin and the future Mensheviks argued against the Economists.

Gramsci defined "economism" in wider terms than other Marxists do, as any trend which downgrades specifically political intervention or assumes that economic developments will (or will unless artificially restrained) mechanically produce corresponding political results. Thus for him laissez-faire ideologies, electoral abstention of any sort, and syndicalism, were all varieties of economism. Gramsci believed that often what has been diffused as "historical materialism" has in fact been "historical economism". He argues that economism tends to lead to:

1. "cheap infallibility" (since everything in a bourgeois society will eventually be accommodated to capitalist interests in one way or another, you can "infallibly" explain all measures as serving capitalist interests)

2. shallow agitation based on exposures of ruling-class individuals' venality, attributing ruling-class policies to "economic" motives in the narrowest sense

3. dialogues with the public in which the "Marxist" takes the role of the "genie with the lamp" exposing the swindles of established leaders to those hitherto too "incurably thick" to register it

4. shallow, passive tactics understating political initiative, and expecting an eventual resolution from iron economic laws which will produce an economic and then a revolutionary-political crisis to be resolved by military force.

FORDISM. The Model T Ford, launched in 1908, was the first car produced in millions and bought by millions. By the end of World War One, almost half the cars on earth were Model Ts.

In 1911 F W Taylor published his book Scientific Management, the first-ever essay in defining "management" as a profession for which people should be trained. He argued that managers should study, plan, and regulate work routines in detail. Before then, workers had generally been trained informally, by older workmates; Taylor argued that managers should take control of training.

In 1913 Ford introduced the world's first moving assembly line. Workers found it a hell-hole. In December 1913, Ford found that his workers stuck it, on average, for only three months. Only 640 of his 15,000 employees had been with the company for three years or more. Worse, trade-unionists from the Industrial Workers of the World were organising in Detroit.

Ford responded by proclaiming the "Five Dollar Day". On top of their basic pay of $2.34, some Ford workers would be paid bonuses bringing them up to the hitherto-unknown rate of $5 a day. That would consolidate a core workforce. At the same time Ford contracted out much work to other companies on much lower wages.

Ford established a Sociological Department to vet the home and sex life of employees to decide who would qualify for the promised $5-a-day wage. Ford also organised evening classes, sports facilities, a company band, and cheap loans. He strongly supported Prohibition of alcohol, which was US federal law from 1919 to 1933. (Chris Reynolds, From Ford to computers, *Workers' Liberty* 11).

But "in the... 1920s the Department's activities were scaled down... The moral element of Ford's labour relations was replaced by 'strong-arm tactics' with gangland overtones" (Ralph Fevre, *The New Sociology of Economic Behaviour*, p.231). These methods kept Ford non-union longer than any other big car company, but eventually in the 1930s the workers unionised the factories.

In his Prison Notebooks, Gramsci saw the defeat of the open revolutionary working-class assault of 1917 and the following few years as being followed by a period of "passive revolution", or "revolution/ restoration", in which the ruling class would find reactionary and bureaucratic ways to respond to the "inherent necessity to achieve the organisation of a planned economy" in place of the revolutionary and democratic way possible if the workers of Western Europe had been able to triumph after 1917.

Fascism was one of the forms of "passive revolution". Gramsci saw Fordism (linked [p.293] to "the liberal state") as another.

Gramsci, in his notes on Americanism and Fordism, was clear that capitalists like Ford "are not concerned with the 'humanity' and 'spirituality' of the worker, which are immediately smashed". He was also clear that Fordism would incubate revolt: the US bosses "have understood that 'trained gorilla' is just a phrase [of Taylor's], that 'unfortunately' the worker remains a man and even that during his work he thinks more..." (than the worker in older industry).

However, in the sense that the most thorough and ruthless capitalist development can also be the most thorough and ruthless incubation of progressive potentialities in the working class, Gramsci also saw "Fordism" as having a greater component of "revolution" in the "revolution/ restoration" couplet than had Italian fascism, dominated as it was in Gramsci's view by a parasitic and mean-spirited petty bourgeoisie lacking technical qualifications and of rural and "rural-type" origin.

The terms "Fordism" and "post-Fordism" have been much talked about since the 1980s. By then the reference point for the concept of "Fordism" was less Gramsci's notes than Michel Aglietta's *A theory of capitalist regulation*, published in 1976.

For Aglietta the history of capitalism was and is a story of the bourgeoisie successively evolving different "modes of regulation". Fordism was one of those, and characterised by assembly-line production; a high development of trade-union collective bargaining, which allowed for rising wages and thus an expanding market for the new production; endemic inflation; economic stabilisation by welfare spending; and a big economic role for the state. What Aglietta meant by "Fordism" was different from what Gramsci meant. Aglietta also sketched a "neo-Fordism" which, by extrapolating from trends of the 1970s, he saw emerging. In the 1980s writers around the Eurocommunist magazine *Marxism Today*, extrapolating in their case from the first period of Thatcherism, sketched a "post-Fordism" on quite different lines.

Technologically, for both Gramsci and Aglietta, "Fordism" was defined by mechanised assembly lines. "Neo-Fordism" (Aglietta) or "post-Fordism" (*Marxism Today*) was defined by automation and computers.

Gramsci's "Fordism" was characterised by a drive to separate off a reliable and high-paid workforce from the rest of the working class, with bonuses a large part of wages, and by union-busting. Aglietta's "Fordism", by a working class more or less unified by national collective bargaining (by unions) and a welfare state.

"Neo-Fordism" was defined by state wage controls and union-bashing, but a trend to unify the working class even more; "post-Fordism", on the contrary, by flexible pay systems using bonuses and a fragmentation of the working class, so that unions were primarily sidelined rather than bashed.

Gramsci's and Aglietta's "Fordism" were both forms of regulated capitalism. Aglietta's "neo-Fordism" was an even more regulated, and statised, form of capitalism; "post-Fordism", on the contrary, was characterised by Thatcherite free enterprise.

"Neo-Fordism" was seen as bringing increased and more generalised class struggle; "post-Fordism", as bringing decreased class struggle and more struggles defined not in terms of class but of varied identities and groupings.

In his notes on the USA, Gramsci assumed that Europe, and Italy in particular, have far larger parasitic and unproductive social strata than the USA.

This may not be true. For example, Gramsci is aggrieved by the large number of lawyers in Italy: 64 per 100,000 population in 1929, a higher rate than elsewhere in Europe. But the USA has far more lawyers: 384 per 100,000 population in 2010. (Italy has become more lawyered-up over the years, but less so than the USA: 205 per 100,000 population in 2007).

The USA also has a hypertrophy of real-estate agents: 234,000 of them in 1930, 190 per 100,000 population, and 644,000 by 1980, 284 per 100,000 population. (Jeffrey M Hornstein, *A nation of realtors: a cultural history of the 20th-century American middle class*, p.207).

Gramsci, it seems, underestimated the vast size of the small-town bourgeoisie and petty-bourgeoisie in the USA. The USA has "31,000 local general-purpose governments with less than 10,000 residents (accounting, with rural areas, for 38 per cent of the nation's population)" http://www.newgeography.com/content/00242-america-more-small-town-we-think.

In his Prison Notebooks Gramsci discussed Sinclair Lewis's novel *Babbitt*, a biting critique of middle-class USA. But he saw European petty-bourgeois derision of Babbitt's philistinism as hollow and hypocritical. At least for the American Babbitt, the petty-bourgeois hero of Lewis's novel, the model to emulate was the industrialist, but for the European "Babbitt" the model was the "canon of the cathedral, the petty nobleman from the provinces, the section head at the ministry" (Buttigieg vol.2 p.356).

But Babbitt is a real-estate agent. He admires his neighbour Howard Littlefield, who is a manager for the city Street Traction Company; but Babbitt had wanted to be a lawyer, and he wants his dopey son Ted to become a lawyer.

Gramsci asserted that the regulation of alcohol consumption and sexual activity attempted by Prohibition in the USA and Ford's Sociological Department is a necessary condition for workers to achieve high productivity with modern technology.

In fact Ford's regulation of his workers' sex lives had fallen away. Gramsci wrote as if he expected Prohibition to return: it was ended (in 1933), he said, "as a result of the opposition of marginal and still backward forces and certainly not because of the opposition of either the industrialists or the workers" (SPN p.279). In fact the American Federation of Labor opposed Prohibition from early on, and from 1931 ran a special campaign committee to contribute to the defeat of Prohibition.

Today, US alcohol consumption today is a bit lower than most West European countries', including Italy's, but only a bit. (On the whole, US states with more industrial development have higher rates of alcohol consumption. Many East European countries average much higher consumption than the USA or Western Europe).

An attempt to compare sexual promiscuity across countries again found the USA to be mid-range, a fair distance behind leaders such as Finland and Israel, but ahead of France and Italy. The USA also has one of the highest divorce rates in the world.

In short, there is no evidence that the patterns of the early 1920s in the USA made for a markedly different long-term trajectory of behaviour there in relation to alcohol and sex; or that teetotalism and strict monogamy are necessary or typical features of more advanced and productive capitalist society.

Over-generalising from Ford's experiment, Gramsci also wrote that in the USA "hegemony is born in the factory and requires for its exercise only a minute quantity of professional and ideological intermediaries". In the USA, he writes: "There has not been... any flowering of the 'superstructure'." (SPN p.285-6)

On the contrary, the USA has long been characterised by the large quantity of "professional and ideological intermediaries" of bourgeois hegemony in the country. Its history shows that such intermediaries are generated by bourgeois society itself, and are not fundamentally residues of previous formations.

The USA developed mass higher education before other countries, and has more university professors than other countries; it was the country above all others where Tocqueville saw "civil society" as having developed, in the sense of a proliferation of voluntary membership organisations; it has long had vast numbers of lawyers and real estate agents, and Jeffrey Hornstein (cited above) sees the role of the real-estate agents as pivotal in the development of a widespread "middle-class" consciousness in the USA; it must have more priests, pastors, and preachers than any other country, and they are politically vocal; and it has (as Engels noted) vast numbers of professional politicians.

Maybe what the USA shows is that a "superstructure" for bourgeois society can allow broad stability in the trajectory of government while itself being quite diversified and variegated. It does not have to have, and may be stronger for not having, the tight unity suggested by Gramsci's term "hegemonic apparatus", and suggested also by the old British catchword, "the Establishment", a nexus of Tory Party, City finance, the Church of England, Oxbridge, and the "public" schools. Thatcher — and, in their time, Lloyd George, Bonar Law, and Baldwin — showed that an aggressive bourgeois policy could be carried through with the help of that nexus but also of disparate elements.

It is the bourgeois state, in the sense of the government and representative structures, which usually ensures continuity and stability in the organising-for-rule of the capitalist class, while allowing diverse groupings to develop around it and influence it. It is possible for the bourgeoisie to reconstitute a shattered government machine, using its less formal networks: the Russian bourgeoisie would eventually have reconstituted a stable government machine, probably fascistic in character, if the Russian workers had not taken power in October 1917. It is easier for the bourgeoisie to replace shattered political parties, media operations, etc. if it retains a more or less stable government machine as pivot.

HEGEMONIC APPARATUS. "In this multiplicity of private associations...", writes Gramsci, "one or more predominates relatively or absolutely — constituting the hegemonic apparatus of one social group over the rest of the population (or civil society): the basis for the State in the narrow sense of the governmental-coercive apparatus".

Peter Thomas summarises Gramsci's view thus: "A class's hegemonic apparatus is the wide-ranging series of articulated institutions (understood in the broadest sense) and practices — from newspapers to educational organisations to political parties — by means of which a class and its allies engage their opponents in a struggle for political power" (*The Gramscian Moment*, p.226).

However, the concept may confuse as much as it enlightens. It may, for a start, be too tied to the conditions of the fascist regime which Gramsci had in mind when he wrote. Under that, a great variety of social institutions were systematically bent to serving "political power"; but, paradoxically, that made the regime more brittle, as a means of capitalist rule, than a developed bourgeois democracy.

a. The biggest voluntary membership organisations in bourgeois Britain are Facebook (30 million), various sports clubs (27 million total), various churches (17.5 million total), the National Trust (3.8 million), the Royal Society for the Protection of Birds (1 million), and the biggest trade unions (NCVO, *UK Civil Society Almanac 2012*). None is a big instrument of bourgeois hegemony (leadership) in society.

b. Even the political institutions of the bourgeoisie (political parties, bodies like the CBI, the media, universities) serve as much to organise and regulate the internal relations in the ruling class and its very large middle-class support network as to secure hegemony over the working class.

c. Compliance in bourgeois society is managed not so much by explicit persuasion but by what Marx called "the dull compulsion of economic relations", copper-fastened by the hold of "commodity fetishism" and the "illusions created by competition". In addition, Gramsci identified political "decapitation" as a third mode of rule besides coercion and consent; functioning bourgeois democracy makes for compliance even when none of the main parties in the bourgeois democracy can gain much positive support. In short, "apathy" or ignorance or resignation — which all require intellectuals/organisers tied to the ruling class to shape them — will do as well to underpin bourgeois rule as positive consent, and may even work "better" in the sense that Machiavelli wrote that it was safer for a prince to be feared than to be loved.

d. We know from Italy in 1992-4 that if the bourgeois state machine perdures, with an authority that accrues to it through "apathy", ignorance, resignation, and sway over communications, then it is possible for the whole political-party apparatus of the bourgeoisie to collapse without bourgeois rule being seriously shaken. Again: for much of the 20th century in Latin America universities had guarantees of autonomy from the government, for example prohibitions on the police or the army entering campuses, and were much more left-wing than the governments wished; yet bourgeois rule remained secure.

e. The working-class socialists cannot use apathy or ignorance or resignation as tools to secure their influence. They must organise. Gramsci was well aware of the asymmetry between working-class socialist striving for hegemony and bourgeois striving for hegemony. "The philosophy of praxis... does not aim at the peaceful resolution of existing contradictions in history and society but is rather the very theory of these contradictions. It is not the instrument of government of the dominant groups in order to gain the consent of and exercise hegemony over the subaltern classes; it is the expression of these subaltern classes who want to educate themselves in the art of government and who have an interest in knowing all truths, even the unpleasant ones, and in avoiding the... deceptions of the upper class and — even more — their own" (FSPN p.395-6). The term "hegemonic apparatus" can obscure the asymmetry.

f. Many politically-weighty voluntary membership organisations of bourgeois democratic society, for example the trade unions, are contested terrain rather than well-adjusted components of a coherent bourgeois or working-class apparatus. Gramsci was well aware of this fact, writing that in the "modern state", "certain forms of the internal life of the subaltern classes are reborn as parties, trade unions, cultural associations" (Buttigieg vol. 2 p.25): maybe he gave it little weight just because his perception was focused on fascist Italy.

g. Even the German Social Democratic Party and the early German Communist Party in their high days, with their workers' libraries, their hiking clubs and sports clubs, their theatre groups, their choirs, and so on, never came near constructing a comprehensive "apparatus" of cultural institutions comparable to that clustered round the bourgeois state, and it is hard to see how a revolutionary socialist party in a capitalist society ever could do that.

HEGEMONY. Leadership. For more on the possible nuances, see Quintin Hoare's note, SPN p.55. For discussion on the many uses and abuses of the term, see the earlier sections of this book, and the item in this Glossary on "Intellectuals, organic and traditional".

HISTORIC BLOC. The term "historic bloc" is sometimes used to mean a "historic" political coalition between social classes. Gramsci, however, used the term with an entirely different meaning: an integral whole combining the material forces and the ideologies in a society (SPN p.377).

HISTORICISM. Gramsci writes of "absolute historicism or absolute humanism" (p.417), and seems to mean by it something like the idea that social reality is nothing other than what history has produced and is producing, and history is nothing other than what human beings produce by their activity in society.

In some passages he seems to extend this thought to the idea that reality is nothing other than what human beings generate by their activity in society, but that is untenable: for example, much of astronomy studies parts of the universe as they were long before human beings existed, because signals from those parts of the universe take so long to reach us.

In some passages, also, he seems to assume a greater degree of collective human awareness about the effects of our actions and how we are shaping society than really exists, or is likely to exist even in a cooperative commonwealth.

A cross-current is added by Gramsci's notes about Ricardo maybe having made a decisive methodological contribution by his use of abstraction ("suppose that..." — mental experiments using simplified models) in economic science. That model-making abstraction has run riot in modern economics, but Marx used it to some degree, evidently believing that there were long-term underlying structures which could be investigated by such a method; and Ricardo (at least) used it more than Smith. For some writers, historicism was all about rejecting that model-making abstraction.

Another cross-current comes from Gramsci's argument about the "dual perspective" and analysing situations on a number of different levels with different timescales. If that is right, then historical events cannot be understood only in the framework of their historical time, because they are simultaneously shaped on a number of different timescales. History cannot be the evolution of a single entity (for Hegel and for Croce, freedom), each stage of which defines the spirit of its particular time.

Gramsci got the phrase "absolute historicism", and probably the very word "historicism", from Benedetto Croce.

Croce, in his turn, meant by the term "historicism" something different from previous writers. He wrote when "historicism" was on the retreat (pushed back by, for example, neo-classical economics) where it had previously been strong, in Germany.

Croce declared that "'historicism' (the science of history), scientifically speaking, is the affirmation that life and reality are history and history alone". He took up Hegel's idea that history is "the story of liberty".

Since the early 19th century "historicism" had been a trend in Germany (the "historical school" of law, the "historical school" of economics, Ranke's history, Dilthey's philosophy, etc.).

Croce, however, used "historicism" to mean philosophical history, the contrary of the German "historicism" which had developed *in opposition to* Hegelian philosophical history.

He disdained "the attempt of the so-called historical school of economics [Roscher and others] to replace deduction and calculation... by an historical comparison of events and economic institutions", and other "historicism" which, he thought, had been only compilation of historical detail, "erudition deprived of thought". (*History as the story of liberty* (1941), pp.65, 84. See also "Historicism: The History and Meaning of the Term", by George G. Iggers, *Journal of the History of Ideas*, Vol. 56, No. 1, Jan 1995, pp. 129-152).

Gramsci located historicism as originating in conservative thought in the period after 1815: "the theoreticians of the ancien regime were in a good position to notice the abstract, ahistorical character of the petty bourgeois ideologies" (i.e. of republicanism, democracy, etc.: Buttigieg vol. 2 p.163). He also criticised Croce as writing "speculative history"; and declared that "Croce's historicism [is]... no more than a form of political moderatism", framed by a fixed assumption that each phase of development continued and conserved progress from the previous phase. (FSPN p.372).

Gramsci's historicism is different both from Croce's philosophical historicism and from the old historical-compilation historicism.

Since Gramsci, the term "historicism" has been given wide currency by Karl Popper's hatchet-job *The Poverty of Historicism* (1961), in which Marx was denounced as being like Hegel and wanting to impose concocted grand laws of historical destiny.

Gramsci's arguments about the impossibility of purely objective historical prediction make him not a "historicist" in Popper's sense.

See also Peter Thomas, "Historicism, absolute", *Historical Materialism* 15 (2007), p.249; "Immanence", *Historical Materialism* 16 (2008), p.239.

INTELLECTUALS AND ORGANISERS. Gramsci equates intellectuals with organisers. This can be sensibly read only as advocacy that adequate revolutionary socialist intellectuals must be organisers, and adequate revolutionary socialist organisers must be intellectuals. (Or rather, must act as intellectuals. "All men are intellectuals", wrote Gramsci, meaning all women and men, "but not all... in society have the function of intellectuals". SPN p.9).

"The mode of being of the new intellectual can no longer consist in eloquence, which is an exterior and momentary mover of feelings and passions, but in active participation in practical life, as constructor, organiser, 'permanent persuader' and not just a simple orator..." (SPN p.10).

"A mass does not distinguish itself, does not become 'independent', without organising itself, and there is no organisation without intellectuals, that is, without organisers and leaders. But the process of creating intellectuals is long and difficult" (Buttigieg vol.3 p.330).

"That all members of a political party should be regarded as intellectuals is an affirmation that can easily lend itself to mockery and caricature. But if one thinks about it nothing could be more exact... The function... is directive and organisational, i.e. educative, i.e. intellectual" (SPN p.16).

The task of the revolutionary socialist party in the working class is not only, or even primarily, to exhort workers to militancy, or to offer organisational resources; it is to educate, in the sense in which the educators can educate only by constantly being educated themselves, and the educated can become educated only by connecting their learning with activity, i.e. becoming educators.

"Clairvoyance is a political value only in as much as it becomes disseminated passion" (SPN p.113).

These passages in the Notebooks take up ideas proposed by Gramsci as practical imperatives as, in 1924, he set to rebuilding the Italian Communist Party from its near-collapse in 1923. (It went down from 40,000 members in early 1921 to only 5,000 in late 1923, and was then rebuilt, painstakingly, under fascist repression, to over 25,000 before the full-scale fascist clampdown at the end of 1926).

"The working class... will for a certain time generally distrust the revolutionary elements. It will... want to test their seriousness and competence...

"In Turin [in 1920] we succeeded in eliminating the reformists from their organisational positions only pari passu as worker comrades, capable of practical work and not just of shouting 'Long live the revolution', were formed from the factory council movement... In 1921 [in the split between the Communists and the old Socialist Party] it was not possible to seize certain important positions... from the opportunists, because we did not have organising elements who were up to the job. Our majority in those centres melted away, as a result of our organisational weakness.

"By contrast, in certain centres, Venice for example, one capable comrade was enough to give us the majority, after a zealous work of propaganda and organisation of factory and trade-union cells.

"Experience in all countries has shown the following truth: the most favourable situations can be reversed as a result of the weakness of the cadres of the revolutionary party. Slogans only serve to impel the broad masses into movement and to give them a general orientation. But woe betide the party responsible if it has not thought about organising them in practice; about creating a structure which will discipline them and make them permanently strong.

"The occupation of the factories taught us many things in this respect" (editorial in the new Ordine Nuovo, 1 and 15 April 1924; *Selections from Political Writings 1921-6*, p.227-8). Gramsci continued that editorial by outlining what he planned to organise in political and theoretical education of the Communist activists.

The idea that adequate revolutionary socialist intellectuals must act as organisers, and adequate revolutionary socialist organisers must act as intellectuals, also links closely with Gramsci's critique of the old Italian Socialist Party.

He wrote of "phenomena of mass betrayal and desertion not witnessed in any other country". The Italian labour movement "produced whole groups of intellectuals who crossed over as groups to the other side" (Buttigieg, vol.2 p.44, p.114).

It was a "paternalistic party of petty bourgeois with a ridiculous sense of self-importance". "Petty intellectuals... formed the organisation of the left" (Buttigieg vol.3 p.41, 119).

In fact the old Italian Socialist Party membership was 90-plus per cent worker and peasant. Gramsci seems to mean that the worker and peasant members were not educated or developed or mobilised to do much more than vote and attend rallies. "The political parties were hardly solid, and they lacked consistent vitality; they only sprang into action during electoral campaigns. The newspapers: their connections with the political parties were weak, and few people read them" (Buttigieg vol.3 p.80).

He sketches a picture similar to that given by James P Cannon of the American Socialist Party before World War One: "Lawyers, doctors, teachers, preachers, writers, professors — people of this kind who lived their real lives in another world and gave an evening, or at most two evenings, a week of their time to the socialist movement for the good of their souls — they were the outstanding leaders of the prewar Socialist Party.

"They decided things. They laid down the law. They were the speakers on ceremonial occasions; they posed for their photographs and gave interviews to the newspapers. Between them and the proletarian Jimmy Higginses in the ranks there was an enormous gulf. As for the party functionaries, the people who devoted all their time to the daily work and routine of the party, they were simply regarded as flunkeys to be loaded with the disagreeable tasks, poorly paid and blamed if anything went wrong..." (*The Struggle for a Proletarian Party*).

Gramsci's answer is also similar to Cannon's: to work constantly at the education of "a middle stratum [in the party] which is as large as possible" (Buttigieg vol.1 p.323) and "a continuous insertion of elements thrown up from the depths of the rank and file into the solid framework of the leadership apparatus" (SPN p.189.

In the old socialist movement there had been an "imbalance between agitation and propaganda... it can also be termed opportunism" (SPN p.227) — that is, "agitationalism", basing the movement on what made easy agitation rather than also developing adequate "propaganda", which in the Marxist terminology of Gramsci's time meant detailed explanation and argument for a relatively knowledgeable audience.

Gramsci argued for making the revolutionary socialist party "monolithic", "rather than base it on secondary questions" (SPN p.158). Other passages in the Notebooks show that he would not have meant "monolithic" in the Stalinist sense, i.e. allowing no scope for debate and minority views. His thought was more like Trotsky's: "The party of the proletariat... is not at all based upon 'such concrete issues'... The proletarian revolutionist, a leader all the more, requires a clear, far-sighted, completely thought-out world outlook. Only upon the basis of a unified Marxist conception is it possible to correctly approach 'concrete' questions" (*In Defence of Marxism*).

Gramsci's critique cuts sharply against the idea that the answer in periods of setback for the socialist movement is to give up on political sharpness, and instead go for "broad", loose, "all-inclusive" parties, based on a few points of current agitation and with the grand questions of socialist politics left in an "agree-to-differ" box. It does not, however, cut against a clear and compact revolutionary socialist organisation, once one has been formed, intervening patiently and constructively in broad and open political formations.

Gramsci stressed the need for "explicative and reasoned (educative) circulars" within the party (SPN p.196) and more generally for putting ideas precisely in writing rather than relying on "rhetorical" or "conversational" answers. However: "unless the editorial boards are linked to a disciplined rank and file movement, they tend to become little coteries of 'unarmed prophets' or to split..."; and warned of "the Sisyphean task of the little periodicals which are addressed to everyone and no-one" (Buttigieg vol.3 p.99).

The apparent supremacy in the old socialist movement of the Marxist theory of the German Social Democracy had been shallow, "merely a phenomenon of abstract cultural influence", because "no organic or disciplinary bonds ensured" it (SPN p.188). Gramsci criticised anarchists because they saw their activity as "as purely 'educative', moral, cultural" rather than taking responsibility for seeking leadership.

The socialist party's educational-organising work has to be polemical — "the philosophy of praxis can only be conceived in a polemical form" (SPN p.421). But it has to be polemic that takes on the best ideologues among our adversaries, and in the strongest form of their argument — at least it must be that "if the end proposed is that of raising the intellectual level of one's followers and not creating a desert around oneself" (SPN p.439).

INTELLECTUALS, ORGANIC AND TRADITIONAL. Gramsci writes of "organic intellectuals" created by the main social classes — for example, capitalist entrepreneurs, technicians, economists, lawyers (SPN p.5) — and "traditional intellectuals", of which he cites ecclesiastics as the prime example (SPN p.7), and who have and consider themselves to have more autonomy.

On closer examination of Gramsci's text, and also, I would argue, in reality, the distinction is very relative. He describes the ecclesiastics as having been organic intellectuals of the medieval landowning class, and of course that the Church's teaching has changed over the centuries, now to accommodate capitalist rather than landowning interests. Conversely, there is a "traditional" element to law: in most cases at least, lawyers consult statute books and case-law, rather than phoning CBI headquarters to find out what they should say. As Engels put it (letter to Schmidt, 27 October 1890): "As soon as the new division of labour which creates professional lawyers becomes necessary, another new and independent sphere is opened up which, for all its general dependence on production and trade, still has its own capacity for reacting upon these spheres as well. In a modern state, law must not only correspond to the general economic position and be its expression, but must also be an expression which is consistent in itself, and which does not, owing to inner contradictions, look glaringly inconsistent. And in order to achieve this, the faithful reflection of economic conditions is more and more infringed upon. All the more so the more rarely it happens that a code of law is the blunt, unmitigated, unadulterated expression of the domination of a class".

In a further complication, trade-union officials, in a developed bourgeois democracy, generally act simultaneously as "organic" intellectuals for *two opposing classes*. They are organically connected with the working class, rise out of it, and to some degree or another advocate working-class interests and organise working-class mobilisation. But they do that within a framework of acceptance of capitalist society, and while (explicitly or tacitly) promoting that acceptance of capitalist society among the working class.

Elsewhere Gramsci gives a slightly different characterisation: "The intellectuals of the historically (and concretely) progressive class" exert a power of attraction and thus generate a "system of solidarity between *all the intellectuals*", welding them into a "caste" (SPN p.60, emphasis added). The term "caste" reads as pejorative, but isn't it just another way of saying a tradition, a frame for research which permits systematic critique and progress beyond individual sallies and speculations?

Gramsci argues in his notes on Bukharin that revolutionary socialists should deal with the strongest arguments of the best intellectuals linked to the ruling class, rather than being content to score points against those who show ruling-class ideology in the worst light (SPN p.432, 439). So revolutionary socialists, organic intellectuals of the working class, must know how to connect (critically) to the traditions of the best bourgeois intellectuals, as Marx did in his time. The working class must break down the division of intellectuals into organic and traditional, to the extent that it really exists.

Arguably, a simultaneous process is always under way on the side of the bourgeoisie, of interconnecting and combining the "organic intellectuals" of the bourgeoisie (capitalist entrepreneurs, managers, etc.) with the "traditional intellectuals" (academics). Hegemony, proletarian or bourgeois, is never just a fact, but always an activity. It is an activity in which the ideas and forms of organisation are constantly being developed, rather than given in advance as direct emanations of class interests; in which there are always cross-cutting "organic" and "traditional" pulls. It always has lacunae and disconnections.

LABRIOLA. Gramsci argued that the best development of Marx's ideas has been by Antonio Labriola. Labriola was the main writer in the Second International on philosophy, after Plekhanov, and the only leading figure in the International with an academic background in philosophy. He came to socialism and Marxism later in life, after first being a liberal Hegelian: he dated his socialist "confession of faith" from 1889, when he was 46. He was generally aligned with the left of the Italian Socialist Party, but in his last years supported talk of Italy seizing Libya, which it did in 1911, seven years after Labriola's death in 1904. Labriola coined the term "philosophy of praxis", emphasised that "the nature of man, his historical making, is a practical process... the history of man is the history of labour", and wrote of a tendential convergence between politics, history, and philosophy. He also, however, decried "the chase after that universal philosophy, into which socialism might be fitted as the central point of everything".

Gramsci wrote that Labriola's contribution had enjoyed a "limited fortune". Some writers such as Croce had "absorbed... certain... elements" of Marxism into an overall idealist (and, in Croce's case, liberal) theory. Would-be Marxists had linked the ideas they got from Marx with, for example, neo-Kantianism, or with "traditional materialism". Gramsci identified Plekhanov (the other main writer on philosophy of the pre-1914 socialist movement, and much respected by the Bolsheviks) as one of those who "relapses into vulgar materialism". (Plekhanov himself, however, praised Labriola's work highly).

Gramsci made a side-swipe at Trotsky's criticism of Labriola, but it is out of place. Trotsky wrote: "Unlike most Latin writers, Labriola had mastered the materialist dialectics, if not in politics — in which he was helpless — at least in the philosophy of history. The brilliant dilettantism of his exposition actually concealed a very profound insight". Labriola's style was aphoristic and unsystematic, and Labriola's attitude on Libya is enough to justify Trotsky's political criticism.

MODERN PRINCE. Gramsci adapts the phrase from the book, *The Prince*, written by the Florentine diplomat Niccolo Machiavelli in 1513-14, at a time when the once-resplendent city states of northern Italy were falling under patchwork foreign domination. Machiavelli's book is a plea for a "prince" who will restore Italy's strength. Unlike all previous writings, *The Prince* discusses politics as something distinct from morality. The prince should gain and keep the goodwill of the people; but he should also be hard-headed, stingy, and where necessary decisively cruel. "Men ought either to be well treated or crushed, because they can avenge themselves of lighter injuries, of more serious ones they cannot; therefore the injury that is to be done to a man ought to be of such a kind that one does not stand in fear of revenge". "All armed prophets have been victorious, and all unarmed prophets have been destroyed". "It is far safer to be feared than loved".

Gramsci also warned that Machiavelli must be understood in his time, very different from now, and that even in his own he ended by putting himself at the service of reaction. Gramsci was not advocating that working-class socialists should copy Machiavelli's recommendations for cruelty and deceit.

Gramsci argues that, despite appearances, Machiavelli developed a sort of "manifesto for the people", a guidebook for those "not in the know" who were "the revolutionary class" at the time, an appeal for the mobilisation of a peasant militia (which would require attention to peasant interests). Machiavelli was a realist, in the sense of basing himself on real forces, and also "a partisan, a man of powerful passions... a creator, an initiator" (SPN p.172). Gramsci set socialists the task of creating a "Modern Prince" with the same combination of qualities.

Repeatedly, and explicitly, Gramsci argued that the "Modern Prince" could only be the revolutionary socialist political party. In his book *The Gramscian Moment* Peter Thomas contends that really, in his last years, Gramsci saw the "Modern Prince" as something more diffuse, in relation to which a revolutionary socialist political party could only be "the tip of the iceberg".

However, in Gramsci's Prison Notebooks trade unions, factory committees, neighbourhood assemblies, workers' defence groups, and other "broader" organisations are mentioned surprisingly seldom, and the great bulk of the allusions to working-class organisation are to parties or to the party press.

That may be in part because Gramsci has in mind, as the actual form of bourgeois polity both in Italy and in increasingly many countries of Europe, a fascist regime in which "broad" organisation is difficult. It cannot be taken as indicating that Gramsci was sectarian; it does make it hard to argue that he was presenting a new scheme in which the revolutionary working-class party would be less central.

ORGANIC CENTRALISM. Amadeo Bordiga, the chief leader of the revolutionary minority in the Italian Socialist Party after World War One and of the Italian Communist Party from 1921 to 1923 (when he was jailed by the fascists), argued that revolutionary socialist party organisation should be based not on "democratic centralism" but on "organic centralism".

The party's strength, said Bordiga, depended not on whether its policies had gained this or that majority vote, but on whether they corresponded to the "invariant doctrine" of revolutionary Marxism.

"Democracy cannot be a principle for us. Centralism is indisputably one... In order to introduce the essential idea of continuity in time, the historical continuity of the struggle which, surmounting successive obstacles, always advances towards the same goal, and in order to combine these two essential ideas of unity in the same formula, we would propose that the communist party base its organisation on 'organic centralism'." (www.marxists.org/archive/bordiga/works/1922/democratic-principle.htm)

Gramsci argued for democratic centralism as "so to speak a 'centralism' in movement — i.e. a continual adaptation of the organisation to the real movement, a matching of thrusts from below with orders from above, a continuous insertion of elements thrown up from the depths of the rank and file into the solid framework of the leadership apparatus which ensures continuity and the regular accumulation of experience..." (SPN p.189).

However, "if the constitutive element of an organism resides in a rigidly and strictly formulated doctrinaire system, one gets a caste and priestly type of leadership. But does the 'guarantee' of immutability still exist? It does not exist... Ideology...[is] something historically produced, as a ceaseless struggle. Organic centralism imagines that it can forge an organism once and for all, something already objectively perfect. An illusion that can be disastrous..." (Buttigieg vol.2 p.56).

Gramsci also argued that organic centralism was linked to a mechanical conception of class struggle, i.e. an idea that the required form of mass working-class mobilisation for which the "invariant doctrine" had provided would be automatically produced by economic developments. It also tended to convert political discourse into a jargon unable to recognise any information or idea not expressed in its own terms as other than a noxious prejudice.

PASSIVE REVOLUTION. Or "revolution/ restoration". Or a process of change managed from above, with the mass of the population passive rather than active.

Gramsci suggested that the French Revolution of 1789-94 had opened up the conditions for and been followed by a wave of more "passive" revolutions elsewhere in Europe (SPN p.114ff). The unification of Italy into a bourgeois state between 1859 and 1870 (ending centuries of disunity and foreign domination) was a "passive revolution": to that fact Gramsci linked what he saw as the "squalor" (SPN p.184-5) of the Italian bourgeois democracy which had in 1922 collapsed to the fascists.

World War One and the Russian Revolution of 1917 had put onto the agenda "the necessity of a planned economy". Fascism in Italy, and maybe Fordism in the USA, were responses to that necessity by way of passive revolution.

PHILOSOPHY OF PRAXIS. By "philosophy of praxis" Gramsci means, more or less, Marxism; but Marxism understood in a particular way, different from the common run of his day. He took the term from Antonio Labriola. Labriola summed it up like this: "the intellectual revolution, which has come to regard the processes of human history as absolutely objective ones, is simultaneously accompanied by that intellectual revolution which regards the philosophical mind itself as a product of history".

Gramsci contrasted his conception with one in which Marxist theory is specialist "sociology", tied to an ages-old philosophical materialism.

For him, "philosophy of praxis" was thought developed beyond "a receptive and ordering activity", or thought which "put the 'will' (which in the last analysis equals practical or political activity) at the base of philosophy". It was "creative" thought "which modifies the way of feeling of the many and consequently reality itself" and which "teaches that reality does not exist on its own, in and for itself, but only in a historical relationship with the men who modify it" (SPN p.345-6).

He also described "philosophy of praxis" as a conception that "does not recognise transcendental... elements but is based entirely on the concrete action of man, who out of historical necessity works and transforms reality" (Buttigieg vol.2 p.378).

SUBALTERN. By subaltern or subordinate classes, Gramsci meant those that were not ruling — generally the workers and peasants in capitalist societies.

TRANSLATABILITY. Gramsci discussed the well-known theme of "the unity of theory and practice" as one of "translatability" between different elements. Thus: "Philosophy — Politics — Economics: If these three activities are the necessary constituent elements of the same conception of the world, there must necessarily be, in their theoretical principles, a convertibility from one to the others and a reciprocal translation into the specific language proper to each constituent element. Any one is implicit in the others, and the three together form a homogeneous circle".

"The philosophy of praxis has synthesised the three movements... the theoretical, the economic, or the political... the unitary 'moment' of synthesis is to be identified in the new concept of immanence, which has been translated from the speculative form, as put forward by classical German philosophy, into a historicist form with the aid of French politics and English classical economics". (Immanence means "dwelling within"; thus in a materialist view ideas "dwell within" material reality, in an idealist view material developments "dwell within" the evolutions of the idea or ideas: SPN p.403, 400).

Elsewhere the three activities "translated" into each other are philosophy, politics, and history. Gramsci's use of "translatability" will have been informed by his own university studies in linguistics and the translation work he did in prison.

He referred to Hegel and to Marx as sources for the idea. The relevant passages from Hegel may be:

History of Philosophy, III/3/B

"Rousseau represented the absolute to be found in freedom; Kant has the same principle, but taken rather from the theoretic side. The French regard it from the side of will, which is represented in their proverb: 'Il a la tête près du bonnet' [he is hot-headed]. France possesses the sense of actuality, of promptitude; because in that country conception passes more immediately into action, men have there applied themselves more practically to the affairs of actuality. But however much freedom may be in itself concrete, it was as undeveloped and in its abstraction that it was there applied to actuality; and to make abstractions hold good in actuality means to destroy actuality. The fanaticism which characterized the freedom which was put into the hands of the people was frightful. In Germany the same principle asserted the rights of consciousness on its own account, but it has been worked out in a merely theoretic way. We have commotions of every kind within us and around us, but through them all the German head quietly keeps its nightcap on and silently carries on its operations beneath it".

III/3/Introduction

"In this great epoch of the world's history, whose inmost essence is laid hold of in the philosophy of history, two nations only have played a

part, the German and the French, and this in spite of their absolute opposition, or rather because they are so opposite. The other nations have
taken no real inward part in the same, although politically they have
indeed so done, both through their governments and their people. In
Germany this principle has burst forth as thought, spirit, Notion; in
France, in the form of actuality".

Here we have a similar idea of parallel developments in France and in
Germany. In France there was the actual revolution. In Germany, where
political and social conditions did not allow a revolution, the animating
ideas of the revolution were elaborated in a more abstract and cryptic
way, by philosophers. Both here and more specifically in the
Phenomenology of Spirit and the *Philosophy of History* Hegel is critical of the
Jacobins and at pains to distinguish his calmer philosophy from them
("the fanaticism which characterized the freedom which was put into the
hands of the people was frightful").

There are asides in Hegel which license the reader to suspect an
element of sarcasm in Hegel's praise for calmer philosophy and an
element of prudence and accommodation in his criticism of the Jacobins.
As far as I know Hegel never made a direct parallel between the Jacobins
and German philosophy.

Gramsci also often refers to a passage in *The Holy Family*, by Marx and
Engels:

"Herr Bruno Bauer based all his arguments on "infinite self-consciousness" and that he also saw in this principle the creative principle of
the gospels which, by their infinite unconsciousness, appear to be in
direct contradiction to infinite self-consciousness. In the same way
Proudhon conceives equality as the creative principle of private property, which is in direct contradiction to equality.

"If Herr Edgar compares French equality with German 'self-consciousness' for an instant, he will see that the latter principle expresses in
German, i.e., in abstract thought, what the former says in French, that is,
in the language of politics and of thoughtful observation.

"Self-consciousness is man's equality with himself in pure thought.
Equality is man's consciousness of himself in the element of practice, i.e.,
man's consciousness of other men as his equals and man's attitude to
other men as his equals. Equality is the French expression for the unity of
human essence, for man's consciousness of his species and his attitude
towards his species, for the practical identity of man with man, i.e., for the
social or human relation of man to man. Hence, just as destructive criti-

cism in Germany, before it had progressed in Feuerbach to the consideration of real man, tried to resolve everything definite and existing by the principle of self-consciousness, destructive criticism in France tried to do the same by the principle of equality".

As I read it, what Marx is saying here is that the political discourse developed in France around the idea of equality — specifically by Proudhon, not by the Jacobins! — had had a somewhat mystified counterpart in Germany, where open political criticism was less possible, in philosophical talk about "self-consciousness".

The point in Hegel and Marx is not really about "translatability", but more about the inability or the failure to translate.

Because the critique based on equality couldn't be translated into German politics, because the critics in Germany couldn't "pass to action", they developed critical ideas "in a merely theoretic way". Even Hegel, the champion of speculative philosophy, says: "in a merely theoretic way. We have commotions of every kind within us and around us, but through them all the German head quietly keeps its nightcap on and silently carries on its operations beneath it..."

Marx refers to the process in the Communist Manifesto, using the word "translate", but in a sarcastic way.

"In contact with German social conditions... French literature lost all its immediate practical significance and assumed a purely literary aspect. Thus, to the German philosophers of the Eighteenth Century, the demands of the first French Revolution were nothing more than the demands of 'Practical Reason' in general, and the utterance of the will of the revolutionary French bourgeoisie signified, in their eyes, the laws of pure Will, of Will as it was bound to be, of true human Will generally.

"The work of the German literati consisted solely in bringing the new French ideas into harmony with their ancient philosophical conscience, or rather, in annexing the French ideas without deserting their own philosophic point of view.

"This annexation took place in the same way in which a foreign language is appropriated, namely, by translation.

"It is well known how the monks wrote silly lives of Catholic Saints over the manuscripts on which the classical works of ancient heathendom had been written. The German literati reversed this process with the profane French literature. They wrote their philosophical nonsense beneath the French original. For instance, beneath the French criticism of the economic functions of money, they wrote 'Alienation of Humanity', and beneath the French criticism of the bourgeois state they wrote 'Dethronement of the Category of the General', and so forth".

By "translation", Marx evidently means here that the German literature was derivative, not that it was equivalent.

Making much of the idea of "translatability" has to depend, I think, on seeing social life as the working-through of a world-view, or as becoming the working-through of a world-view, so that the world-view and political and historical developments are "translations" of each other. Gramsci, indeed, writes that "many idealist conceptions... may become 'truth' after the passage" [i.e. the socialist revolution]; that "absolute idealism... could become 'truth' after the transition from one realm to another" (Buttigieg vol.2 p.188); and that "the foundation of a directive class... is equivalent to the creation of a Weltanschauung" [world view], which suggests that once the class has been formed by economic processes and established its world-view, its rule is then equivalent to the working-through of that world-view. (There are hints of this idea also in some of Gramsci's passages about the ruling class's "hegemonic apparatus", with which both the apparatus of government and social life become closely aligned).

But even when conscious human control of social life is much greater than now, after a socialist revolution, people will differ and get lots of things wrong. Technological developments, and many natural developments, will be grossly unpredictable. Any "translation" between philosophy and politics and history (social life in movement) will at best be like the sort of Google translation that, going from English to Welsh to Vietnamese then back to English, transforms "The history of all hitherto existing society is the history of class struggles" into "History of the entire social history is so far the class struggle".

UNITED FRONT. At the origin the "united front" was a particular tactical innovation of the Communist Parties, epitomised in an Open Letter issued by the Communist Party of Germany on 8 January 1921 calling on the Social Democrats and other workers' organisations to join with the Communist Party in united action on workers' economic demands, for defence against right-wing gangs, and to free worker political prisoners. In 1921-2 and later the Communist Parties developed it into a general approach of seeking united action of all workers' organisations on practical matters of common concern, while continuing to criticise and indeed expecting that the reformists would probably at some point pull back and thus substantiate the communists' criticisms vividly. The term "united front" is sometimes used more loosely to mean alliance of differing working-class and socialistic tendencies in common practical struggle combined with free mutual criticism.

WAR OF POSITION AND WAR OF MANOEUVRE. In the first few years after World War One, revolutionary socialist energies in Europe were geared to assembling strong communist parties and taking the offensive for soviet (workers' council) power as soon as possible. Incipiently in *Left-Wing Communism* (1920), and more sharply in the advocacy of united-front tactics from 1921 (see "united front"), Lenin, Trotsky, and other Bolshevik leaders argued, eventually with success, for a turn to more patient and sinuous tactics, geared in the first place to winning larger or majority support in the working class by action on more immediate and detailed demands.

The Italian Communist Party resisted the turn to united-front tactics longer than others, and Gramsci was in the midst of the debate, especially after he went to Russia for the 4th Congress of the Communist International in mid-1922. In many passages of the Prison Notebooks he discusses the turn through military analogy — war of position and war of manoeuvre — and muses about the relative roles of such phases in 19th century bourgeois politics.

The analogy works poorly. The usual military terms are "war of attrition" and "war of manoeuvre". "Warfare by attrition pursues victory through the cumulative destruction of the enemy's material assets by superior firepower... Examples of warfare with a high attrition content are... the operations of both sides on the Western Front of the First World War... US operations in Korea after 1950; and most US operations in the Vietnam War.

"On the opposite end of the spectrum is warfare by manoeuvre which stems from a desire to circumvent a problem and attack it from a position of advantage rather than meet it straight on... Instead of attacking enemy strength, the goal is the application of our strength against selected enemy weakness... Examples of warfare with a high enough manoeuvre content that they can be considered manoeuvre warfare include German Blitzkrieg operations of 1939-1941, most notably the invasion of France in 1940; the failed Allied landing at Anzio in 1944, which was an effort to avoid the attrition battles of the Italian theatre..." (US Marine Corps, *Warfighting*, MCDP 1, 1997, pp.36ff).

Direct analogues of war of manoeuvre — surprise assaults at weak points of the enemy — can have little part in a socialist revolution which mobilises the mass of the working class to oust and replace bourgeois power at every level. As Engels put it in his 1895 Introduction to Marx's *The Class Struggles in France*: "The time of surprise attacks, of revolutions carried through by small conscious minorities at the head of masses lacking consciousness is past. Where it is a question of a complete transformation of the social organisation, the masses themselves must also be in on it, must themselves already have grasped what is at stake, what they are fighting for, body and soul. The history of the last fifty years has taught us that. But in order that the masses may understand what is to be done, long, persistent work is required..."

The October 1917 revolution was mostly not "war of manoeuvre".

Political tactics analogous to military war of manoeuvre can be used only in relatively small-scale struggle — lightning-fast industrial strikes, "flash mob" demonstrations, surprise workplace occupations, guerrilla warfare. It may play a bigger role under very repressive regimes (as with Luddite tactics in the repressive conditions of the Napoleonic wars) than in more liberal conditions.

Gramsci himself noted that: "comparisons between military art and politics, if made, should always be taken... with a pinch of salt... In political struggle, there also exist other forms of warfare apart from the war of movement... or the war of position... Another point to be kept in mind is that in political struggle one should not ape the methods of the ruling classes" (SPN p.484-5).

The term "war of position" may have encouraged people in the Communist Parties from the 1950s to think of activity geared to winning official posts (municipalities, union leadership posts) as good "Gramscian" tactics. The gist (poorly) indicated by the analogy is that revolutionary socialist policy has phases of steady and relatively low-key tactics, and others of fast-moving open confrontation.

Some people read some passages from Gramsci's Prison Notebooks as saying that in Western Europe only steady, low-key tactics can ever be viable, and even suggesting that socialist revolution can come through such tactics alone. That Gramsci did not intend that message is shown by his discussion of how to analyse relations of forces, where he flags up the "politico-military" level of direct confrontation as well as the straight political.

The military analogy is more confusing than helpful. Of value in Gramsci's notes which use the analogy is the light they shed on how steady and relatively low-key tactics can be made imaginative and varied, and avoid lapsing into opportunism.

The main works referred to are:

Anderson, Perry, 1976. "The Antinomies of Antonio Gramsci". New Left Review I/100 [AAG]
Gramsci, Antonio, 1957. The Modern Prince and other writings. International Publishers, New York
Gramsci, Antonio, 1971. Selections from the Prison Notebooks. Lawrence and Wishart, London [SPN]
Gramsci, Antonio, 1977. Selections from Political Writings, 1910-1920. Lawrence and Wishart, London
Gramsci, Antonio, 1978. Selections from Political Writings, 1921-1926. Lawrence and Wishart, London
Gramsci, Antonio, 1995. Further Selections from the Prison Notebooks. Lawrence and Wishart, London [FSPN]
Gramsci, Antonio, 2011. Prison Notebooks (ed Joseph Buttigieg). Columbia University Press, New York [Buttigieg]
Thomas, Peter, 2010. The Gramscian Moment. Haymarket Books, Chicago. [GM]

The references in the Glossary are within the text, rather than footnoted. Footnoted references for the rest of the book:

[1] "The Revolution Against 'Capital'", Selections 1910-1920, p.34
[2] FSPN, p.355
[3] "On the L'Ordine Nuovo Programme", Selections 1910-1920, p.291
[4] Ibid, p.293
[5] "Unions and Councils", Selections 1910-1920, p.100
[6] "Political Capacity", Selections 1910-1920, p.349 (translation adapted: Gramsci used the term "little men", but reflecting the usages of the time, not a desire to exclude women)
[7] "Editorial from Ordine Nuovo", The Modern Prince, p.19
[8] "On the L'Ordine Nuovo Programme", Selections 1910-1920, p.293-4
[9] "Towards a Renewal of the Socialist Party", Selections 1910-1920, p.191, 195
[10] Trotsky, Leon, 1971, The Struggle Against Fascism in Germany. Pathfinder, New York: p.191
[11] "The Italian Situation and the Tasks of the PCI ('Lyons Theses')", Selections 1921-1926, p.368
[12] SPN, p.236

[13] SPN, p.238
[14] "The Southern Question", The Modern Prince, p.31
[15] "The Southern Question", The Modern Prince, p.32
[16] "The Southern Question", The Modern Prince, p.36
[17] FSPN, p.16
[18] FSPN, p.304
[19] SPN, p.429, 438
[20] SPN, p.323
[21] SPN, p.185
[22] SPN, p.147
[23] FSPN, p.395-6
[24] GM, p.226
[25] GM, p.163
[26] GM, p.194
[27] GM, p.xxii
[28] GM, p.436
[29] GM, p.291
[30] Adorno, Theodor, 1966. Negative Dialektik. Suhrkamp, Frankfurt: p.144
[31] GM, p.438
[32] SPN, p.152
[33] AAG, p.43
[34] AAG, p.46
[35] AAG, p.61ff
[36] AAG, p.22, 31
[37] AAG, p.40
[38] AAG, p.26
[39] GM, p.48
[40] GM, p.53-4, 61, 170
[41] GM, p.93-4
[42] http://bit.ly/nineham, viewed 17/12/12
[43] GM, p.137-8
[44] GM, p.138
[45] GM, p. 144
[46] GM, p.193
[47] GM, p.191
[48] GM, p.162
[49] GM, p.163
[50] GM, p.194

[51] GM, p.237

[52] GM, p.224

[53] GM, p.226

[54] GM, p.220

[55] GM, p.198

[56] GM, p.186-7

[57] Trotsky, Leon, 1971, The Struggle Against Fascism in Germany. Pathfinder, New York: p.394

[58] Lenin, Vladimir Ilyich, 1964. Better Fewer But Better, in Selected Works, volume 3. Progress, Moscow: p.715

[59] Trotsky, Leon, 1971, The Struggle Against Fascism in Germany. Pathfinder, New York: p.158-9

[60] GM, p.225

[61] Bellamy, Richard, 2001. "A Crocean Critique of Gramsci on Historicism, Hegemony and Intellectuals", Journal of Modern Italian Studies, Vol. 6, No. 2, pp. 209-229

[62] Chantal Mouffe interviewed by Dave Castle, Red Pepper, June 1998

[63] Marx, Karl, 1970. Critique of the Gotha Programme, in Selected Works, volume 3. Progress, Moscow: p.26

[64] Fiori, Giuseppe, 1990. Antonio Gramsci: life of a revolutionary. Verso, London: p.252-3

[65] Rosengarten, Frank, 1984-5. "The Gramsci-Trotsky Question", Social Text #11

[66] Trotsky, Leon, 1953. The First Five Years of the Communist International, volume 2. New Park, London: pp.220-22

[67] Serge, Victor, 1963. Memoirs of a Revolutionary. Oxford University Press, London: pp.186-7

[68] "Letter to Togliatti, Terracini, and Others", Selections 1921-1926, p.192

[69] "On the Situation in the Bolshevik Party", Selections 1921-1926, p.432

[70] SPN, p.238

[71] Zinoviev, quoted from The Lessons of the German Events, p.44-45, in James, C L R, 1937, World Revolution 1917-36, Furnell, New York: chapter 12

[72] SPN p.236

[73] Trotsky, Leon, 1953. The First Five Years of the Communist International, volume 2. New Park, London: pp.196-7

[74] Ibid p.260

[75] Trotsky, Leon, 1975. The Mistakes of Rightist Elements of the

Communist League on the Trade Union Question, in Leon Trotsky on the Trade Unions. Pathfinder, New York: p.34

[76] SPN, p.165

[77] SPN, p.146

[78] Trotsky, Leon, 1975. A Necessary Discussion with our Syndicalist Comrades, in Leon Trotsky on the Trade Unions. Pathfinder, New York: p.9

[79] Trotsky, Leon, 1975. Writings of Leon Trotsky, 1929. Pathfinder, New York: p.193

[80] Trotsky, Leon, 1979. Leon Trotsky on France. Monad, New York: p.223

[81] SPN, p.153

[82] Trotsky, Leon, 1975. The Challenge of the Left Opposition. Pathfinder, New York: p.203

[83] SPN, p.429

[84] SPN, p.171

[85] SPN, p.439

[86] SPN, p.332-3

[87] Trotsky, Leon, 1974. The Third International After Lenin. New Park, London: p.61-2

[88] Trotsky, Leon, 1976. Writings of Leon Trotsky 1937-38. Pathfinder, New York: p.439

[89] Trotsky, Leon, 1979. Leon Trotsky on France. Monad, New York: p.95-6

[90] SPN, p.167-8